Make Work Meaningful

How To Create a Culture That Leaves a Legacy

Prina Shah

Host of the *Ways to Change the Workplace* Podcast

Ways to Change the Workplace Press

Copyright © 2024 by Prina Shah

Make Work Meaningful: How to Create a Culture That Leaves a Legacy

First published in 2024 by Prina Shah

All rights reserved. No part of this book may be reproduced or used in any manner without written permission of the copyright owner except for the use of quotations in a book review.

Book Cover Design and Interior Formatting by 100 Covers.

ISBN: 978-1-7635734-0-6 (paperback)

ISBN: 978-1-7635734-1-3 (ebook)

ISBN: 978-1-7635734-2-0 (audio book)

Papa kehte hain bada naam karegi, Beti hamari aisa kaam karegi

Well, more my Mum actually.

And I did it – my way!

For Mum and Poppa

Contents

About Prina Shah ix
Welcome – Watch This Video First! xiii
This Book is For... xiv
How to Use This Book – Guide to Implementing
  the Activities xvii
What do I mean by legacy? xix
A Note to Self Before You Start Reading xxi

PART 1 of Make Work Meaningful: Discovering Your Legacy

**Chapter 1: The Missing Piece - The Achievement
and Legacy Paradox** 3

You've Got the Job, Now What? 3

Case Study: My Journey 4

From Ambition to Meaning 5

Crafting Your Legacy 6

Activity: The Achievement and Legacy Paradox
Questions 7

**Chapter 2: Discovering Your Rudder -
Your Underlying Purpose** 15

Staying True to Your Core 15

Case Study: The Rudderless CEO 17

The Unseen Power of Soft Skills 18

Examples of People at Work Struggling with

Staying True to their Core Values: 20

The Missing Piece 22

So How and Where Do You Begin? 23

Activity: Qualities Self-Assessment 24

Chapter 3: Designing Your Legacy Goal 27

More Than Just a Career 27

Case Study: Sh*t Sticks 28

Activity: Consider Your Current Culture
When Making Change 31

Activity: Define Your Legacy Goal to Make Work
More Meaningful 35

PART 2 of Make Work Meaningful:
Creating a Culture of Legacy

Chapter 4: Defining Your Desired Culture 43

The Importance of a Desired Culture 43

Case Study: The Clear Communicator CEO 44

Activity: Defining Your Desired Culture Workshop 48

Chapter 5: Effectively Conveying Your Desired Culture 59

The Power of Marketing Principles 59

Know, Like and Trust Marketing Principles
Explained for Culture Change 61

Case Study: McDonald's Know, Like, and Trust 63

Apply Know, Like and Trust Principles to
Your New Desired Culture 66

Activity: Checklist for Deconstructing
Know, Like, and Trust Principles 67

Chapter 6: Building a Solid Team 73
The Importance of Teamwork 73
Case Study: The Burnout Checklist 74
Activity: How to Identify Lone Ranger (Silo) Teams 77
How to Unify Your Team.. 81
Activity: Reflect on Your Team's Achievements........................... 82

Chapter 7: Building Alliances 91
The Power of Alliances 91
Case Study: You'll Never Walk Alone 91
Choosing Not to Walk Alone 93
Activity: Self-Assessment of Professional Alliances 95
Side Note: Who Do You Advocate For?
How To Be an Ally.. 100
Reflective Activity: Novel Ideas for Building
Inclusive Networks and Advocacy.. 101

Chapter 8: Leading with Head, Heart, and Backbone 107
The Balance of Leadership... 107
Case Study: New Levels, New Devils 108
How To Lead with Head, Heart, and Backbone....................... 109
Activity: Head, Heart, and Backbone Self Assessment 112

PART 3 of Make Work Meaningful: Sustaining Your Legacy

Chapter 9: Culture Optimisation Beyond Surveys 123
Beyond Surveys 123
Case Study: Anthony Vuleta's Way 125

Making Moments That Matter 129

Activity: Reflective Questions on Optimising Culture 135

Chapter 10: Managing Plot Twists **139**
Navigating the Unexpected 139

Case Study: Common Career Plot Twists 142

Activity: The Revolutionary Act of Weekly
Self-Coaching to Keep Your Legacy Goal in Check 144

**Chapter 11: Knowing When to Leave
and Pass the Baton** **149**
Recognising When to Leave 149

Activity: Knowing When to Leave Questions 154

Case Study: Effective Knowledge Transfer 155

Bonus Activity: Knowledge Transfer Plan 157

Chapter 12: The Show Will Go On **163**
The Continuation of Legacy 163

Fictional Case Study: John's Journey to Creating a
Meaningful Legacy 165

Activity: Reflective Questions on Ongoing Legacy 169

Acknowledgements **173**
Ways to Work with Prina **175**

About Prina Shah

Prina became disillusioned with the workplace early in her career, so she decided to learn the ropes and rejig the system. In this book are the key learnings from her direct experiences with clients.

Prina has over 20 years of experience in human resources (HR) and is one of those rare people who has straddled both sides of HR. She has worked in generalist HR to put out fires and she has specialised in organisational development to enable proactive HR practices. Prina has a wealth of leadership experience and talks from her own lived experience where she has managed large HR teams and turned them around to be high performing.

Prina specialised in organisational culture change and individual behaviour change in her corporate days. Since leaving the corporate world and starting her own business, she has worked with many organisations around the world to optimise their cultures and their people.

Seeing the same issues repeat over and over again in her career, Prina knows there is a better way forward. This book contains the tried and tested steps of that 'better way'.

This book is a practical guide for you to make work more meaningful. To take charge of the legacy and organisational culture that you wish to create and leave.

Prina has a Bachelor of Science in Sociology and Social Psychology from Loughborough University in the UK. And a Diploma of Professional Coaching from the Australian Institute of Management. *She also has a Bachelor of Arts in Contemporary Art — that is a story for another time.*

Prina owns a global consultancy business where she helps organisations to optimise their cultures and their wonderful employees.

Prina also hosts a podcast called Ways to Change the Workplace where she speaks to thought leaders from around the globe about how to make work better. Subscribe and tune in to the Ways to Change the Workplace podcast via your podcast provider.

Early in life, Prina saw the direct negative impact work has on a person through her Poppa (Dad). As a migrant he had it tough. He brought his stress home, and the whole family felt it.

Prina is the daughter of Anil and Neeina and sister to Manisha. She was born in Mombasa and is a second-generation Kenyan. Prina was brought up in the UK from the age of eight. Her formative years were in the UK. She fell in love with an Australian, Lindsay, in 2013 and moved to Australia in 2014. She now lives in stunning Perth, Western Australia.

Prina likes to do something scary every year. Prina was a glassblower's assistant for a year. She is left-handed and everything glass related is right-handed, there was a lot to learn! During her career in human resources, she felt a need for something more, so she studied (and aced) a degree in contemporary art. She used to be a practising contemporary mixed media artist. She has done a comedy class and a stand-up comedy set, and abseiled down a 52-storey building for charity. Prina believes there is more to life than work, but while we are at work we may as well make it a good place to be.

We spend more of our day at work than we do with our loved ones, we have to make work meaningful, not just for ourselves, but for others too.

Prina loves a good bad joke, food and travel – if you want her to speak to, or develop your teams and people, get in touch! If we work together muchos laughter and serious conversations are guaranteed.

Prina's email is prina@prinashah.com and she wants to know how this book has served you. Prina's full details are on the back page. Get in touch.

Welcome – Watch This Video First!

Here is the link to the video I would love you to watch before you begin reading this book:

https://www.makeworkmeaningful.shop/

Join me, Prina Shah, in uncovering your brilliance and how you can make work more meaningful and leave your legacy.

Together, we will learn how to make a mark that transcends job titles and resonates with more of the essence of your soul. That is what the world needs more of, right? Let's leave legacies that will resonate long after you have moved on *and* during your work life. Why wait until the end? You can leave a legacy every day.

> "Most of us have two lives.
>
> The life we live,
>
> and the unlived life,"

says Steven Pressfield in his book, *The War of Art*.

This is what I want to address in this book. *The unlived life that we have in the workplace.*

This book, "Make Work Meaningful: How to Create a Culture That Leaves a Legacy." is your guide to transforming the way you approach work, ensuring that every step you take is towards creating a lasting, positive impact.

Drawing from my own experiences, the experiences of my clients and the stories of others, this book provides practical strategies and activities to help you align your career with the intention of creating a meaningful culture that thrives beyond your time.

This Book is For...

- Executives, leaders and teams who feel there is more to their workday than simply clocking in and out.
- Those who want to leave the workplace in a better state than when they arrived.
- Those who want to make work more meaningful.
- The dreamers, visionaries and change agents who wish to leave a legacy at work, whatever stage and age they are in their career – they know there is something more.

More about this book:

- It is a practical guide for you to work on as an individual or as a team.
- It is your work companion.
- It will challenge you.
- It will develop you beyond your expectations if you apply all the learnings.
- This book will help you to leave a ripple effect of positive change for the better that will impact those around you now and in years to come. Who knows what impact your efforts will have on those who follow.
- Some stories in this book have been amended with poetic licence so as not to break the confidentiality of the case studies that I mention.

How to Use This Book
Guide to Implementing the Activities

Lay the groundwork

If you are working on this solo, carve time out in your diary to ensure you complete each activity.

If you are working as a team, set up a meeting and make sure everyone has the necessary materials and mindset. I recommend you meet after each chapter to decide how you will put the learnings into place.

When it comes to mindset, consider the standards you expect. For example, when I kick off executive team coaching, we set up mutually agreed mindset ground rules along the lines of: we commit to delivering, we respect each other's opinion, we will be creative and not shut down new ideas. And the best one, *we will have fun along the way.*

I want you to have fun along the way with this book.

The materials you will need as you read the book are a pen and paper. There are notes sections at the end of each chapter. If you want to capture your own notes, have a notepad dedicated to this book. Or get creative as a team and see what shared channels you can use at work.

How can I use the book?

Read each chapter to gain a thorough understanding of the forces at play, then apply the activities per chapter to suit your needs.

If you are time-poor, or dying to make your changes, you are welcome to jump straight to the activities to get immediately into it.

Execute the activities

Either solo, or by leading a discussion to extract valuable insights from the team, decide how you will capture the learnings.

By integrating these activities into your work, you will significantly enhance team collaboration and productivity.

Depart with a roadmap

However you capture the insights, be sure to assign action items and document the plan for moving forward.

It is going to be super practical.

What do I mean by legacy?

By legacy I mean the lasting impact and influence you leave behind in your professional sphere through your actions, contributions, decisions, and relationships. It encompasses positive changes, upheld values, and inspiration provided to others.

Legacy isn't solely about grand achievements or recognition; it's about the meaningful difference you create and the mark you leave. It's aligning work with deeper purpose and values, striving to better the world. Legacy is the result of a purpose-driven career journey, extending beyond personal ambition to create lasting impact.

Another way I look at it is;

- What do I want people to remember me by after I have left this job?
- How do I want people to talk about me?
- How do I want people to think about me?
- How do I want people to feel about the work I did and have left behind?
- How do I want my work and impact to others to be described as when I move on from this company and this industry?
- Or perhaps your work will result in an anonymous legacy, one you may not be aware of, but one that affects people positively long after you have made your mark.

We need to find better ways to change the workplace. That is why I called my podcast Ways to Change the Workplace!

The purpose of this book is to provide a practical guide as you move through various jobs during your career. I have tried and tested all the activities mentioned in this book.

The activities at the end of each chapter are designed to serve as your guide to make the changes that you need to make at work.

This book is a lifelong tool for your career. It can be applied to the future jobs that you move to.

Let's make work meaningful!

A Note to Self Before You Start Reading

- **Remember:** This book will help you to leave a ripple effect of positive change for the better that will impact those around you and those in years to come.
- **To do:** Either fold down the corner of this page or bookmark it to return to your notes at the end.
- **Situation:** I am reading this book because:

- **Your First Move:** What is the first step I can take today to start making work meaningful?

- Turn Your Knowledge Into Action:
    - ☐ Read this entire book.
    - ☐ Study the activities outlined in this book and apply them.
    - ☐ Accept that the road ahead won't be easy, but it will be a fun and wild ride!
    - ☐ Don't stop when you are tired but do have a rest.
    - ☐ Stop when you have accomplished your mission.
    - ☐ When you move to another job, read this book and apply the learnings again.

Sign (Your signature): _____

Keep me posted! My email is prina@prinashah.com. I want to know how this book served you. Get in touch via email or via socials.

Cheering You On:

Prina (*helping you find excellent ways to change the workplace*) Shah

PART 1 of Make Work Meaningful: Discovering Your Legacy

CHAPTER 1

The Missing Piece - The Achievement and Legacy Paradox

> **Chapter Overview**
>
> In this chapter, we explore a common yet often unspoken feeling: the sense that something is missing even after achieving career success. There is still that nagging feeling that something vital is missing deep within us. Sometimes that feeling is loud, sometimes that feeling lurks quietly in ourselves. This is what we call the achievement and legacy paradox. By the end of this chapter, you'll understand this paradox better and begin your journey towards making your work truly meaningful.

You've Got the Job, Now What?

Congratulations! You've landed your dream job or you're on the fast track to getting there. This should be it, right? The pinnacle of your career, the crowning glory after years of burning the midnight oil, climbing the ladder, and pushing through every obstacle. So why is there that gnawing feeling deep inside, telling you something crucial is missing?

You're not alone. Many reach the summit of their careers only to find themselves staring into an unsettling void. It's an uneasy feeling that's hard to put into words. Even Gallup's annual survey, The State of the Global Workplace, picks up on this vibe. Terms like "quiet quitting" and "presenteeism" float around, hinting at the same restlessness that you might be feeling right now.

Think about it. You're expected to bask in your accomplishments, to feel that surge of pride. After all, you've sacrificed so much: late nights, tough conversations, missed family events. This should be a moment of unbridled joy, yet something feels off. Despite your success and the accolades, the jubilation you anticipated is elusive. You're left wondering why the pinnacle of your success doesn't feel as fulfilling as you imagined.

It's baffling, isn't it? You've checked all the boxes, hit all the marks, and yet, something's missing. The high you expected to come with your success is just out of reach. You're left in a swirl of confusion, introspection, and maybe even frustration, wondering why this pinnacle doesn't feel as satisfying as you imagined.

Case Study: My Journey

I questioned my packed days, back-to-back meetings and team achievements. What was I doing it all for? I was stuck in a pit of approving memos, responding to emails and trying to find time after my meetings to do the actual work I had to deliver. After I moved on, someone else would come along and reinvent the wheel. As proud as I was of my, and my team's, successes in public, internally I felt "meh." Something was still missing, and I went in search of it by quitting my corporate job, and starting my consultancy business during the pandemic. I took the leap. My mum and everyone else around me freaked out. I was so sure in myself that there was something more, and I haven't looked back

> *since... There is something more and this is what I am covering in this book.*

Back to you... This is the moment to dig deep and ask yourself the hard questions. What's truly missing? What is it that you're really seeking? This feeling isn't just a fleeting doubt; it's a signpost, guiding you to something more profound, something that goes beyond just achievements and titles.

You've reached a point where you need to rethink what success means to you. Is it just about the next promotion, the bigger office, the larger pay cheque? Or is it about something deeper, something that resonates with your values and passions? Faced with the achievement and legacy paradox, it's time to shift from chasing success to creating significance. The missing piece lies in the impact you make, the legacy you leave behind.

So, let's get real. What kind of mark do you want to leave on your field, your team, your organisation, and the lives you touch? It's time to move from ambition to meaning, from success to significance. It's time to find that missing piece and make your work meaningful.

From Ambition to Meaning

The missing piece is your connection to the impact you aspire to make. It's not about being a Nobel Prize winner; it's about making a difference in your world. It's an intangible element that many leadership programmes overlook. It's about something greater than just your individual success. Internally, I knew there was something more.

> *For me, internally, I knew there was something more to do. As Dr. Wayne Dyer says in his book The Shift, I was ready to move from "ambition to meaning"!*

> *I felt an emptiness during my corporate career. Despite all the outward signs of success, I felt unfulfilled. I realised that my ambitions had driven me to achieve, but they hadn't guided me towards significance. It was time for a change. Dr. Wayne Dyer's concept of moving from "ambition to meaning" really resonated with me. It was a turning point that made me see that true fulfilment comes from making a meaningful impact.*

For this book, we'll use this concept of ambition to meaning to delve into your career aspirations and explore the legacy you wish to create. It's not just about climbing the ladder but understanding why you're climbing it and how your ascent can make a difference. *It's about shifting your focus from personal gain to collective good, from success to significance.*

You're ready to move from ambition to meaning, from chasing success to creating a lasting impact. Let's discover how to turn your achievements into a legacy that resonates far beyond your immediate sphere. This is where true fulfilment lies—beyond the accolades and into the heart of meaningful impact.

Crafting Your Legacy

Your legacy is the mark you leave on your field, your team, your organisation, and the lives you touch. It's about your values, vision, and commitment to something larger than yourself. This legacy is more than professional achievements; it's a narrative of your contributions to bettering your community, industry, and society.

Consider the story of Maya Angelou. Her legacy goes far beyond her literary achievements. She was not just a poet, an author, and a singer; she was a beacon of resilience, a voice for the voiceless, and a tireless advocate for justice and equality. Maya Angelou used her talents to challenge societal norms and inspire millions. Her work resonated deeply, touching hearts and minds across generations.

Imagine if Maya Angelou had focused solely on her immediate success and recognition as a writer. Her words might still have been powerful, but her legacy would not have been as profound. Instead, she aligned her work with a greater vision of social justice and human dignity, creating a lasting impact that goes beyond her literary contributions. Her legacy is felt not just in her books, but in the lives she touched and the changes she inspired.

Your legacy should have depth and reach. It's not just about the immediate results of your work, but about the enduring impact of your vision and values. It's about creating something that outlasts you, something that continues to inspire and improve the world long after you're gone.

As you reflect on your career, think about the stories people will tell about you and your work. Will they talk about your titles and awards, or will they speak of the difference you made in their lives and in the world? Aim for the latter. Strive to build a legacy that is not just remembered but felt deeply by those who follow in your footsteps. This is where true fulfilment lies—beyond the accolades and into the heart of meaningful impact.

Activity: The Achievement and Legacy Paradox Questions

As I said above, I've been there. This exact funk – the achievement and legacy paradox – hit me during my corporate career. Here's what it means:

While we're laser-focused on achieving our career goals—climbing the ladder, earning the promotions, hitting the targets—we often neglect to consider the lasting impact we want to make. We get caught up in the hustle, the metrics, the next big milestone. We become so engrossed in the pursuit of success that we forget to think about what comes after. This relentless focus on achievement can leave us feeling hollow, as if something crucial is missing.

I vividly remember the days when I should have felt on top of the world. I had the titles, the recognition, the so-called success. But inside, I felt a growing sense of emptiness. My days were filled with back-to-back meetings with minimal loo and lunch breaks, relentless targets, and an endless to-do list. I was achieving, yes, but to what end? Was I making any meaningful difference? Was I creating something that would last beyond the immediate results?

It was in those moments of introspection that I had my "aha" moment. I realised that success isn't just about reaching the top; it's about what you do as you get there and the difference you make along the way. It's about shifting from a mindset of mere ambition to one of meaningful impact. This realisation was the catalyst for me to redefine my career.

Reflecting on Your Journey:

For this activity, as you reflect on your career, think about where you currently stand and where you want to go.

People generally fall into one of four categories in their professional journey: Legacy Leaders, Legacy Feeders, Legacy Believers, and Legacy Dreamers.

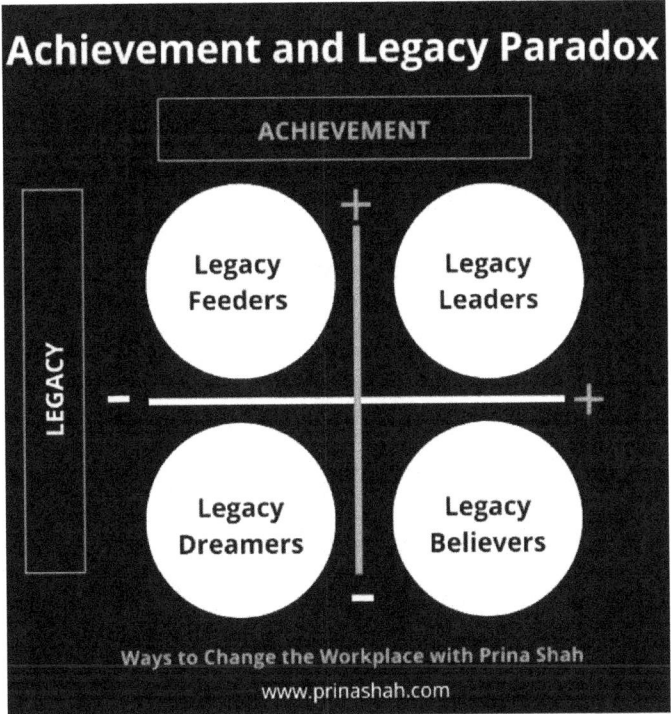

Above is a diagram to highlight the stages of the achievement and legacy paradox. Understanding where you fit and where you need to move to can help you navigate towards a more meaningful work life. Try this activity...

Legacy Leaders

Legacy Leaders have achieved remarkable success in their careers and have also left a meaningful and enduring impact on their field. They balance their achievements with a vision for lasting change. Think of Bill Gates, who not only co-founded Microsoft but also dedicated himself to philanthropy through the Bill & Melinda Gates Foundation, tackling global challenges like health and education.

Questions to Consider:

- Have I achieved remarkable success in my career?
- Do I believe I've left a meaningful and enduring legacy in my field?
- Am I actively balancing my achievements with a vision of a lasting impact?
- Do I aspire to positively influence the workplace, my industry, my community, and the world through my contributions?
- Does my journey reflect a harmonious coexistence of success and a meaningful, enduring legacy?

Legacy Feeders

Legacy Feeders are high achievers who have reached a point of significant success in their careers and now yearn to create a lasting impact that goes beyond their immediate accomplishments. Think of Sheryl Sandberg, who, after achieving significant success with Facebook (now Meta) has used her platform to advocate for women in leadership and created the Lean In movement.

Questions to Consider:

- Have I achieved significant success in my career?
- Do I yearn to create a legacy that outlasts my immediate accomplishments?
- Have I dedicated my time, energy, and resources to ascend my career ladder to achieve my legacy-building goals?
- Have I defined what legacy I want to leave?

- Am I actively working on bridging the gap between my high achievements and the enduring legacy I desire?
- Is my career marked by both success and a growing desire for a lasting imprint?

Legacy Believers

Legacy Believers prioritise creating a lasting legacy and have made significant strides in that direction. They might not be at the pinnacle of their professions yet, but their focus is on making a meaningful impact. Think of Tim Cook, who, while leading Apple after Steve Jobs, has continued to innovate while also placing an emphasis on sustainability, privacy, and ethical manufacturing practices.

Questions to Consider:

- Do I prioritise creating a lasting legacy?
- Have I made significant strides in building a legacy?
- Do I understand the significance of leaving a lasting impact on the lives I touch?
- Is my focus directed towards creating a legacy that resonates through time?
- Am I a visionary who dreams big and works diligently to turn those dreams into reality?
- Have I defined the career success I wish to reach?
- Am I starting to achieve success in my career?

Legacy Dreamers

Legacy Dreamers are at an early stage, aspiring to both career achievements and leaving a legacy. They recognise the need for growth and are on a journey of self-discovery and improvement. Think of a young Richard Branson in the early days of Virgin. Branson aimed to disrupt the music industry with Virgin Records and has since expanded to various sectors, focusing on broader issues like space travel through initiatives like Virgin Galactic. As a Legacy Dreamer, you are in a similar position. You are laying the groundwork, driven by both ambition and a desire to make a meaningful difference. Reflect on your passions and the impact you want to have.

Questions to Consider:

- Do I aspire to both career achievements and leaving a legacy?
- Do I acknowledge that I've yet to make significant strides in either realm?
- Have I recognised the need to elevate my professional achievements and focus on the legacy I wish to create?
- Do I harbour the potential for improvement and a willingness to evolve?
- Am I actively seeking to balance my journey towards greater achievement and crafting an enduring legacy?
- Do I believe that there is more to my workday than clocking in and out?

Reflect on your answers to identify where you are in relation to being a Legacy Leader, Legacy Feeder, Legacy Believer, or a Legacy

Dreamer. The purpose of this book is to help you navigate from where you are to where you want to be, turning your achievements into a meaningful legacy.

And as you turn the page, get ready to dive deeper into understanding how to transform your ambitions into lasting impact. Let's redefine what success means and create a legacy that resonates far beyond the walls of your office, cubicle or desk.

Your efforts to make work meaningful starts now.

Chapter Recap

In this chapter, we've explored the achievement and legacy paradox, understanding that achieving career success doesn't always equate to meaningful fulfilment. The paradox highlights the need to align your achievements with a vision of a lasting legacy to make work meaningful.

Your Actions:

- ☐ Go back to the beginning and write to your future self if you have not yet done so on the page provided under the title "A Note to Self Before You Start Reading."
- ☐ Complete the achievement and legacy paradox questions.
- ☐ Reflect on what you need to address to move through the achievement and legacy paradox stages.
- ☐ Prepare for the next chapter, where we'll delve into discovering your rudder, a.k.a. your underlying purpose or driving motivation.

Notes:

CHAPTER 2

Discovering Your Rudder - Your Underlying Purpose

> **Chapter Overview**
>
> Sometimes we try to please everyone, and we end up pleasing no one. In this chapter we cover a case study of a fictional CEO who was in such a situation. We explore the concept of your rudder, which represents your underlying purpose or driving motivation. By the end of this chapter, you'll have a clearer understanding of your core values and how they guide your actions and decisions at work.

Staying True to Your Core

Aesop's fable, "The Miller, His Son, and Their Ass," tells the story of a miller and his son trying to please everyone as they journey to the market with their donkey. Initially criticised for letting the son walk, then for both riding, and finally for carrying the donkey, the miller realises the impossibility of pleasing everyone. The moral emphasises the futility of conforming to ever-changing opinions and highlights the importance of authenticity. In our workplaces, this fable is a powerful reminder of why staying true to our core values is crucial.

In the corporate world, opinions are everywhere, and trends change with the wind. No doubt your executive team experiences what I call "brain farts" — impulses to jump on the latest craze out of excitement or fear of missing out. We've all been there. It happens when we don't have our internal compass set to chart the right course.

Self-actualisation, which sits at the peak of Maslow's hierarchy of needs, is one of the hardest things for most to achieve. It represents the realisation of our full potential and the desire to achieve personal growth, self-improvement, and creative expression. It means pursuing our passions, talents, and aspirations, striving for peak experiences and self-fulfilment. It involves a deep sense of purpose, autonomy, and authenticity, as well as a commitment to continuous learning and personal development. This is the profound "know thyself" work that the philosopher Plato spoke of.

When we fail to reach self-actualisation, we end up with piecemeal work, half-hearted projects, a disengaged workforce, and an internal sense of just band-aiding problems as we drift through our careers, constantly chasing the next shiny thing.

Think about it. How often do you find yourself bending over backwards to accommodate the latest trends or the loudest voices, only to feel disconnected from your own values? This disconnection can lead to a kind of professional emptiness, where despite all outward appearances of success, something crucial is missing.

Staying true to your core means aligning your actions with your values, even when it's challenging. It's about making decisions based on what truly matters to you, not just what's expected or what seems popular at the moment. This alignment brings a sense of integrity and fulfilment that goes beyond superficial achievements.

Remember, it's not about reaching some final destination of success; it's about how you travel and the impact you make along the way. Your core values are your guideposts, helping you navigate through the noise and stay focused on what truly matters. When your actions reflect your true self, you bring authenticity to your work, inspire those around you, and build a legacy that resonates deeply.

Reflect on your own journey. Are you making choices that align with your core values, or are you drifting along with the currents of external expectations? It's time to reset your compass and chart a course that stays true to who you are. This is the foundation of a meaningful and impactful career.

Case Study: The Rudderless CEO

Imagine a CEO who had achieved great technical success and climbed the corporate ladder to the top. (I will use a mix of examples of a number of CEOs whom I have supported. This is a fictional case study). However, they struggled with aligning their personal values with their leadership role. This misalignment led to stagnation and dissatisfaction. By focusing on their core values and realigning their actions with their underlying purpose, they were able to regain their direction and lead with authenticity.

This fictional CEO lost their voice. They had landed their role thanks to their technical expertise, being promoted throughout their career to the next level. However, the board noticed something was off and brought me in to support the CEO. Let's refer to them as the rudderless CEO.

People get to a certain stage in their career, and others notice something isn't quite right. Whether you're a manager or an employee, your peers, team, or leaders might start giving you feedback on areas you need to elevate in your career. These are often described as soft skills, which are ironically quite hard to develop.

When you haven't developed your soft skills or your core values, things often misalign.

The Unseen Power of Soft Skills

Soft skills, often sidelined as secondary, are in fact the unsung heroes of effective leadership. They are the subtle, yet powerful abilities that drive meaningful interactions and foster a thriving workplace culture. Unlike technical skills that can be easily measured and quantified, soft skills require a nuanced understanding of human behaviour and emotions. This is what makes them so elusive and challenging to master.

Empathy: Consider empathy, the ability to understand and share the feelings of others. It's more than just listening; it's about genuinely connecting with your team's experiences and perspectives. Empathy allows leaders to build trust and foster an environment where employees feel valued and understood. It's the difference between being a boss and being a leader who inspires loyalty and commitment.

Communication: Effective communication is another cornerstone. It's not just about conveying information clearly; it's about engaging in a dialogue that encourages open exchange and mutual respect. Good communicators are able to navigate difficult conversations, provide constructive feedback, and articulate a compelling vision that motivates and unites their team.

Adaptability: In today's rapidly changing business landscape, adaptability is crucial. Leaders must be able to pivot and respond to new challenges and opportunities with agility. This requires a mindset that is open to change and a willingness to embrace uncertainty. Adaptable leaders are not only resilient but also innovative, continuously seeking ways to improve and stay ahead.

Emotional Intelligence: Emotional intelligence (EI) ties many of these soft skills together. It's the ability to recognise, understand, and manage our own emotions while also being attuned to the emotions of others. High EI enables leaders to handle stress, navigate conflicts, and maintain a positive work environment even in the face of adversity.

Conflict Resolution: Effective conflict resolution is a critical skill that involves addressing disagreements in a constructive manner. Leaders with strong conflict resolution skills can mediate disputes, find common ground, and facilitate solutions that respect all parties involved. This skill not only prevents workplace tensions from escalating but also strengthens team cohesion.

Developing these soft skills requires intentional practice and a commitment to personal growth. It's about being curious about yourself and others, seeking feedback, and being willing to step out of your comfort zone. It's about understanding that leadership is not just about the goals you achieve but how you achieve them and the relationships you build along the way.

For the rudderless CEO, regaining their direction meant diving deep into these soft skills, aligning them with their core values, and leading from a place of authenticity. It's a transformative process, one that turns managers into inspiring leaders who can navigate their teams through both calm and stormy waters.

As you reflect on your own career, consider how these soft skills play a role in your professional journey. Are there areas where you can grow and develop? Remember, the most impactful leaders are those who balance their technical expertise with the power of soft skills, creating a legacy that is both successful and deeply human.

Examples of People at Work Struggling with Staying True to their Core Values:

Consider the below examples in light of the soft skills which may be missing.

The CEO Focused on Short-Term Gains: A CEO who prioritises immediate financial targets over long-term vision, compromising company values and employee morale in the process. This leads to short-term wins but long-term instability and dissatisfaction among the workforce.

The Manager Prioritising Personal Ambition: A manager who, in their drive to climb the corporate ladder, neglects team development and well-being. This creates a high-stress environment, leading to burnout and high turnover rates.

The Emerging Leader Overwhelmed by Change: An emerging leader tasked with driving organisational change, but who fails to communicate effectively and support their team through transitions. This results in resistance, confusion, and a decline in team cohesion and productivity.

The Seasoned Professional Resistant to Innovation: An experienced professional who struggles to adapt to new technologies and methodologies, clinging instead to established ways of working. This resistance hinders their career growth and impacts the organisation's ability to innovate and stay competitive.

Are you feeling similar sentiments in your career? Are you unknowingly holding yourself back? Are you potentially missing your internal guide?

Returning to the Rudderless CEO...

This fictional CEO is well regarded in their industry, boasting a history of numerous career successes. Now, the Board is relying on this CEO to take more of a visionary lead. Unfortunately, the CEO finds themselves in a state of stagnation. Despite their best efforts, they express a feeling of being stuck. They've made significant strides in ensuring board and employee support: The CEO has diligently worked to guarantee the Board and employees feel supported, regularly keeping them informed about crucial updates and key organisational information.

However, the missing parts were these areas:

Strategic Decision-Making: Decisions were made based on the loudest voice in the executive room, out of fear of disappointing them and receiving passive-aggressive vitriol.

Crisis Management: Crisis management was left to the technical experts with good intentions, but no timely decisions were made, as the CEO forgot that the buck stops with them.

Effective Communication: Important messages were passed on through internal channels that many field staff didn't log into, leading to a communication void and resentment. It was a case of "check the intranet."

Talent Development and Retention: People were left to develop themselves in areas misaligned with the organisation's growth, resulting in a lack of coherent talent development.

Self-Promotion and Professional Brand: The CEO invested no time in professional branding, networking, and image management, losing contact with their network and peers.

Long Game Focus: The CEO focused on immediate fixes, always working in a reactionary firefighting mode, neglecting a long-term visionary view.

Do you see what happened here? It's the classic tale of a well-intentioned, highly capable person who is also a people pleaser. By ensuring everyone is content here and now, and managing immediate challenges, they neglected crucial elements necessary for sustained growth and success, leading the Board to question their leadership.

My focus was to guide the CEO towards a more balanced and strategic approach to leadership, incorporating a long-term vision while addressing immediate needs. The goal was to help the CEO navigate challenges while building a foundation for sustained success and growth. The CEO had lost their rudder—their inner guide.

Are You the Same?

One thing I've seen repeatedly is that when someone starts a new job, they often have a 90-day to 12-month plan to hit their given milestones. You are going to achieve these milestones nonetheless, whether you have a grand plan or not. Truth is, the systems of your workplace—from one-on-ones, setting your objectives, to paying you—will all ensure that you are ticking the right corporate boxes. The ecosystem of a workplace is made to ensure that you achieve.

The Missing Piece

What I'm alluding to is the missing piece… Whether you are a people pleaser or not, there are aspects of your inner self that you may not have considered for your career and legacy longevity. This missing piece is your connection to the impact you aspire to make. It's not about making change on a global scale; it's about making a difference in *your* world. It's an intangible element that many leadership programmes overlook. It's about what's greater than just your individual success.

The missing piece is recognising and aligning with your core values and purpose. It's the difference between merely climbing the ladder and understanding why you're climbing it. It's about creating a legacy that goes beyond personal achievements and touches the lives of others. This deeper connection is what transforms your work from a series of tasks into a meaningful contribution.

For me, this realisation was a turning point. I felt this emptiness during my corporate career. Despite all the outward signs of success, I felt unfulfilled. My ambitions had driven me to achieve, but they hadn't guided me towards significance. It was time for a change.

So How and Where Do You Begin?

We can start by looking at what we know, by observing and learning from those we admire. Think about your mentors, coaches, great past leaders, and the like. The people who stand out to you in your career thus far. Those who have that special something—not just professional achievements, but the intangible qualities that make them exceptional.

Reflect on those mentors, coaches, and past leaders who have left a lasting impression on you. What is it about their character that resonates with you? Is it their unwavering commitment to their values, their ability to inspire and motivate, or their skill in navigating challenges with grace?

As we explore these qualities, we're not merely listing them as abstract concepts. Instead, we're seeking to understand how these qualities manifest in the real world, in the actions and behaviours of those you admire. It's about distilling the essence of leadership qualities and considering how they can be cultivated within yourself.

This external exploration serves as a rich source of inspiration and learning for our deeper internal needs. By examining the qualities that have contributed to the success and impact of others, we pave the way for a more profound understanding of our own aspirations and potential.

Activity: Qualities Self-Assessment

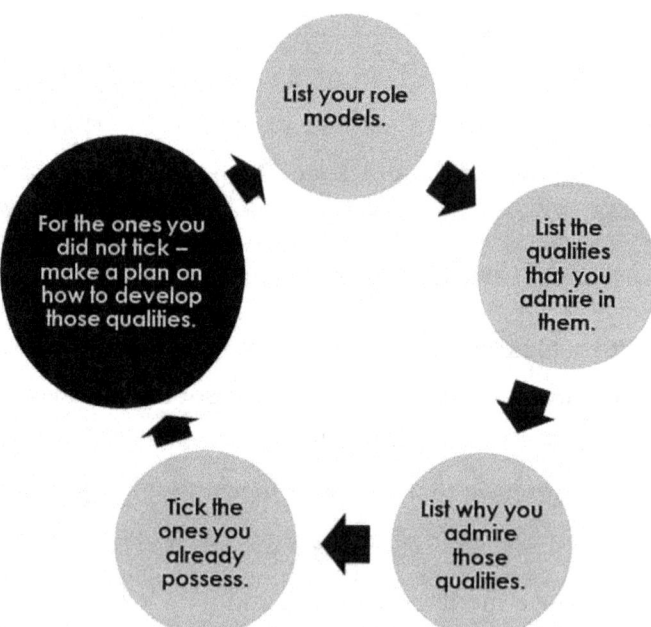

Reflect on the following questions to identify the qualities you admire in others and wish to develop in yourself:

- List your role models, mentors, and leaders who have inspired you.
- Identify the qualities, the soft skills and characteristics that you admire in them.

- Determine why you admire these qualities.
- Tick the qualities you already possess.
- Make a plan to develop the qualities you do not possess.

> **Chapter Recap**
>
> In this chapter, we've explored the importance of staying true to your core values and understanding your underlying purpose. By reflecting on the qualities you admire in others and developing these qualities in yourself, you can ensure that your actions align with your purpose.
>
> **Your Actions:**
>
> - ☐ Complete the Qualities Self-Assessment.
> - ☐ Create your development plan.
> - ☐ Prepare for the next chapter, where we'll delve into designing your legacy goal.

Notes:

CHAPTER 3

Designing Your Legacy Goal

> **Chapter Overview**
>
> In this chapter, we shift our focus from immediate achievements to the long-term impact you want to leave. This chapter encourages you to consider more than the organisation and strategic goals. You will consider what your personal intention is in relation to your efforts at work and provide you with tools to start crafting your legacy. By the end of this chapter, you'll have a clearer understanding of the legacy you wish to leave

More Than Just a Career

In our careers, we often focus on short-term goals like achieving KPIs or hitting targets. But what about the long-term impact you want to leave? What about your legacy? This chapter is about shifting your focus from immediate achievements to the lasting mark you want to make in your professional sphere.

Are you driven or have you been dragged through your career? Remember the achievement and legacy paradox I covered at the beginning?

It is the paradox of many a high achiever's career path. The climb to the top (whatever the top is for you) can be arduous and intense, with personal aspirations and external expectations both propelling you forward. Yet, as you reach this peak, you may realise that it's not merely about the destination or the job title, or about your place in the hierarchy anymore, but it is more about the legacy you now want to leave behind.

That's your recap on the achievement and legacy paradox.

You may currently have, or had, a 90-day plan for all you wanted to achieve when you started your new job. Or you have your current key performance indicators and your performance goals set for the organisation.

But what about YOU and your own grand plans?

Did you ever have a longer-term plan for what you want to leave in terms of a legacy at work?

Here's a story for you about someone without a thought as to what legacy they wished to leave at work…

Case Study: Sh*t Sticks

Let me share a cautionary tale. This person won't be named as the case study is one that we can all learn from.

This person was a self-made corporate success story. They didn't have a degree, which in their mind they felt held them back, and they worked multiple jobs to make ends meet when they started their career.

Fast forward through years of toil, long nights, extra study and not seeing their family much; they carved out an international career to finish as a Chief Financial Officer and part owner of the company! Wow.

Their accolades surpassed their expectations. But let's go back a little…

This person was a high-flying corporate whizz kid in their career.

A key milestone was winning a job abroad, which included family relocation.

It was the opportunity of a lifetime. One that would change their career, and which has impacted the foundation of their kids; growing up in a foreign land and experiencing so much that they would never have got to do if it wasn't for their whizz kid parent.

The whizz kid was known for being ruthlessly efficient. They were recruited for that very reason.

In their new job, they were on a mission. They had their 90-day plan to make efficiencies for the organisation; to impress the bosses, to impress the board, and to save a lot of money for the organisation.

However, this whizz kid missed some crucial pieces of the puzzle: the people, the culture of the workplace, and the legacy the whizz kid wished to leave.

While they made excellent corporate efficiencies and saved lots of money, the whizz kid didn't win the hearts and minds of their people.

In fact, the whizz kid was nicknamed the 'Cereal Killer' by their people.

Why?

Because, as an efficiency measure, they stopped morning breakfast foods being provided to employees.

The whizz kid saved a lot of money.

It made corporate sense.

But it made zero sense to their people (and for the organisational culture).

Their people used to arrive early in the morning, have their breakfast together, mingle and get on with the day. It was their thing. An unsaid way of connecting with each other.

What the Cereal Killer forgot to notice is that this breakfast time was an important time to their people; that they came in early to work just to catch up with each other.

It was a part of their collective unspoken organisational culture. An informal routine or tradition – which is exactly what happens in societal culture if you look at religion, for example. People create their own cultural patterns; going to Mecca, the Wailing Wall, attending the Kumbh Mela, doing the Camino de Santiago Walk or in this case… gathering in the morning over breakfast to mingle and connect with each other.

Once the cereal was gone, so were the people, and so was their culture.

Nobody turned up early for work anymore.

They worked their allocated hours and went home, detesting the Cereal Killer.

There are a couple of lessons to this story.

- Expand your radar to your people and the current culture when making change.
- Consider the legacy you want to leave before you make any big or small decisions like cancelling the corporate breakfast perks.

I want to cover both of the above points. Let's begin with the first one.

Activity: Consider Your Current Culture When Making Change

Before making any changes, it's crucial to understand your current culture and expand your radar to the current reality of what you are working with. Many well-intentioned people don't consider the below aspects before defining the changes they wish to seek and make at work. Use the following framework to assess your organisation.

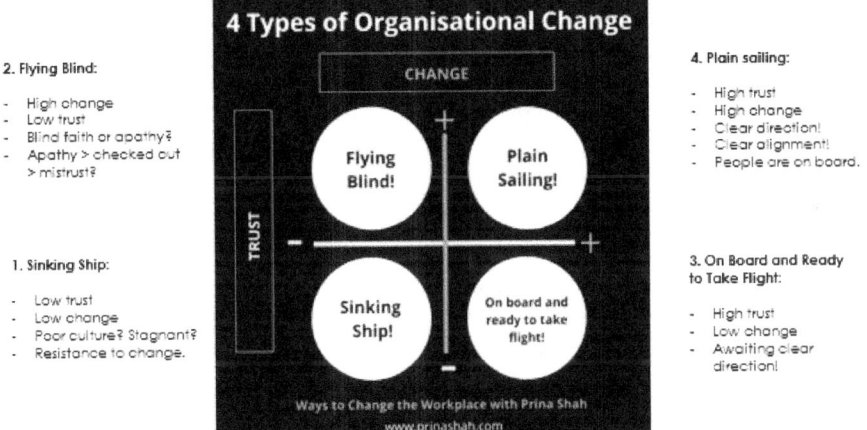

Consider where your organisation is placed...

Above is a framework outlining four types of organisational change with an axis of change against trust. I want to outline the organisational culture that is attributed to each quadrant.

Is your organisation a Sinking Ship?

- Do you have low trust and low change?
- Is your organisational culture poor or stagnant?

- Is there resistance to change?

Is your organisation Flying Blind?

- Do you have high change, but low trust?
- Is there blind faith or apathy to your change efforts?
- Have people checked out? Or is there mistrust?

Is your organisation On Board and Ready to Take Flight?

- Is there high trust, but low change?
- Are your people now awaiting clear direction?
- Is the leadership team resisting making change / decisions?

Is your organisation Plain Sailing?

- Is there high trust and high change?
- Is there clear direction?
- Is there clear alignment?
- Are your people on board?

Using the above information, determine where your workplace culture is at.

My workplace is:

☐ A sinking ship

☐ Flying blind

☐ Plain sailing

☐ On board and ready to take flight

You have now assessed the reality of your workplace culture. You will no doubt have lots of thoughts from this activity. Record them here so you remember what you need to consider: _____

_____
_____
_____
_____
_____

If the Cereal Killer had considered the above activity prior to making changes, I wonder what decisions they would have made differently.

They would have understood the nature of the culture that they were dealing with and could have decided accordingly.

This is also about reading the room and applying discernment beyond your immediate ambitions. It is about moving you on from ambition to meaning.

Consider this… The Cereal Killer could have done the above activity and learned that the organisational culture wasn't ready and that perhaps they were in the Flying Blind category. They had high change, but low trust which usually results in apathy to your change efforts. And therefore, if a "bad" decision is made, people may well check out and mistrust the decision maker.

If the Cereal Killer had had that revelation, they could have handled the situation better and in return they would have left a better legacy than forever being referred to as the Cereal Killer by their jesting family.

They could have gone back to the executive and told them that while it is expensive to provide breakfast to workers, the benefits of it are that they arrive early and immediately get to work after eating. I bet they worked longer hours; they could have factored that into their calculations. They could have understood and explained that the employees had good camaraderie, so to make a drastic decision on the cereal situation would result in lesser performance as well as having a negative cultural impact.

What executive would say no to that sound decision?

Sh*t sticks and it certainly did in the form of the Cereal Killer nickname in this case.

Consider the legacy you want to leave before you make any decisions, big or small.

Many great people that I coach had not yet considered the legacy they wish to leave.

Considering the legacy you wish to leave requires tapping into yourself, not into the corporate agenda.

Considering the legacy you wish to leave requires asking yourself some tough questions which might require you to think and be different going forward.

This part is going to make you potentially uncomfortable.

This part is going to remind you of your mortality. SPOILER ALERT: We all have an expiry date.

Identify which category your organisation falls into and consider the implications for your legacy.

Activity: Define Your Legacy Goal to Make Work More Meaningful

The next part will enable you to delve deeper. I have used the acronym of LEGACY to lay out the core concepts for your consideration: Longevity, Essence, Genuine, Awareness, Consequences and Yearning.

First reflect on these questions and then in the next section, define your legacy goal:

L - Longevity:

- How do my decisions contribute to the longevity of positive impact?
- What learnings can I extract from past decisions to shape my legacy?
- What specific actions today align with the legacy I aspire to leave?

E - Essence:

- How can I ensure my leadership embodies the essence of my authentic self?
- In what ways can I explore and express my unique qualities at work?
- How can I envision a legacy that transcends my current role and responsibilities?

G - Genuine:

- Are my intentions and decisions consistently genuine and sincere?
- How can I guard against compromises that may deviate from my core values?
- What guiding principles ensure authenticity in my leadership decisions?

A - Awareness:

- How does my awareness of time's finite nature impact my choices?
- Can I cultivate acceptance of uncomfortable truths for personal growth?
- In what ways can I align my actions with the inevitability of an expiry date?

C - Consequences:

- How often do I contemplate the long-term consequences of my decisions?
- How can my actions of today contribute positively to the workplace over time?
- What decision-crafting strategies can uphold a positive legacy?

Y - Yearning:

- Do I yearn for personal and professional transformation in my leadership?

- How can I yield to discomfort as a catalyst for meaningful change?
- In what areas can I evolve to align with my legacy aspirations?

Declaring the legacy you aspire to leave isn't just an exercise; it's your first step towards crafting a meaningful workplace. This declaration isn't just a formality – it's your North Star, keeping you aligned with your highest career aspirations. It's the fuel that keeps you motivated to create the legacy you genuinely desire.

Embrace this process wholeheartedly, as it has the power to transform your professional life and positively impact others too. So go ahead, declare your legacy, and let it resonate in every action you take.

What is Your Legacy?

Your legacy starts with your declaration. Remember to tag me or contact me so that I can celebrate with you. My details are on the last page.

Write down your answers and reflect on them regularly.

Overall, the legacy I wish to leave at work is…

I wish to: _____

_____
_____
_____
_____

so that (be sure to expand upon this and if you get stuck try 'so that' again and again after you get your first answer, go deeper as per my example). _____

_____

Make Work Meaningful

_____
_____
_____
_____

As an example, here is mine:

I wish to: *find decent ways to change the workplace* ***so that:*** *people, their families, communities, and societies* <***so that***> *are happier* <***so that***> *and not impacted negatively by the crappiness of work that people take home.*

Chapter Recap

The story of the Cereal Killer in this chapter illustrated the need to align your efforts with the organisational culture. It highlights the need to meet people where they are at. The legacy questions to ask yourself section enables you to consider the bigger picture in relation to how you intend to leave your legacy at this job. We've discussed the importance of designing a legacy goal and considering the cultural impact of your decisions. By reflecting on the legacy questions, you can start to shape a meaningful and lasting impact in your professional life.

Your Actions:

- ☐ Complete the quadrant exercise provided and consider your current culture prior to making any change.
- ☐ Be sure to always keep your current culture in mind when making changes.
- ☐ Ask yourself the LEGACY questions.
- ☐ Define your legacy goal to make work more meaningful.
- ☐ Prepare for the next chapter, where we'll delve into designing your desired culture.

Notes:

PART 2 of Make Work Meaningful: Creating a Culture of Legacy

CHAPTER 4

Defining Your Desired Culture

> **Chapter Overview**
>
> Defining your desired culture is something many don't do due to not knowing how. A desired culture is different to that of your current culture. A desired culture is what you strive to create. This chapter provides you with a case study of a CEO that I worked for. He was one of the most direct people in terms of his communication and clear vision for his desired culture. We'll explore the difference between current and desired culture and provide you with practical tools to articulate and embed this vision within your organisation. By the end of this chapter, you'll have a clear understanding of the culture you wish to create and how to achieve it.

The Importance of a Desired Culture

The last chapter was about tapping into yourself and your drivers, soft skills, motivators and qualities to help you to leave a lasting legacy. It also helped you to assess where your current workplace culture sits.

This chapter now focuses on the legacy you wish to leave with your organisation, your division, or your team in the culture or subculture that you wish to create.

You may have read the many definitions of workplace culture which range from it's the way we do things around here, our organisational DNA, to a set of shared values, norms and beliefs. Whatever it is defined as, it is essentially the vibe of your workplace. It is the feeling one gets after working there for a week.

That is your current culture; it is alive and kicking.

A desired culture is different from your current culture. It represents what you aspire to create within your organisation, division, or team. Without a clear vision of your desired culture, your efforts may lack direction and purpose.

A desired or aspirational culture is a definition of the way forward. It is clarity on how your organisation, division or team will be, look and feel like in ? amount of years. A desired culture is usually something to aspire to in the next three to five years.

If your organisation hasn't articulated its desired (or aspirational) culture, it lacks a clear future-focused goal for itself and its teams. Without a defined desired culture to strive for, your organisation may feel directionless and lacking in purpose.

I also want to help you to create a good subculture if you do not have influence over the overall organisational culture. You can still impact your division or your team with what you are about to read/learn… Consider whether you are working on this at an organisational or a team level.

Case Study: The Clear Communicator CEO

I worked with a CEO who was very direct and clear with his language. He consistently reinforced his vision for the organisation with the phrase "Enjoy the day and be the best that you can be." This clear and consistent communication helped embed the desired culture within the organisation, with employees adopting and applying this mindset in their daily work.

This CEO was very direct and clear with his language, whether it be in person or via writing. It seemed like he had a marketing guru help to develop his professional brand and voice.

His emails were always signed off as, "Enjoy the day and be the best that you can be."

A clear behavioural call to action.

When I first started working with him, I was slightly perturbed by such a statement at the end of every email from him. Why would he state that? Wasn't it obvious? (The statement might appear glaringly apparent, yet to others, a consistent reminder could prove invaluable. This is marketing 101 for leaders – repeat your message over and over and over).

After a while, I discovered the intent behind his communication style – it was a relentless commitment to clarity. The repeated mantra at the conclusion of each email and each all-staff meeting wasn't a mere afterthought; it was a deliberate act setting clear expectations.

Through this, he was charting a course for all, urging everyone to, "enjoy the day and be the best that you can be," in their own unique way.

What surprised me further after a few weeks of working with this CEO, is people in the organisation would utter the same (or similar) phrase as the CEO. When a hiccup happened during a project, leaders asked the team, "how can we be the best that we can be given this hurdle? How do we overcome it?" My ears pricked up. Hello, people were repeating the CEO's language and applying it to the way they were leading their work and the way that they were leading others.

People would say it in relation to the projects they led, or the teams that they managed, or the way they dealt with difficult workplace circumstances; their collective aspiration was to, "enjoy the day and to be the best that [they could] be!"

We all need clear direction and expectations. Studies and many culture survey tools have found in the workplace that one needs clear role outlines, clear guidelines on how to belong to the organisation, and we all need transparent consequences for deviating from established expectations. Yet many workplaces lack such basic principles in defining, creating and managing their culture/s at the organisational, divisional or team levels.

Here are specific examples of what the CEO achieved:

Established a Clear Professional Brand: The CEO collaborated with internal communications to create a distinct professional brand and voice, ensuring clarity and consistency in all internal and external communications.

Emphasised a Clear Call to Action: Every email from the CEO ended with the signature sign-off, "Enjoy the day and be the best that you can be." This phrase acted as a behavioural prompt, highlighting personal accountability and motivation.

Demonstrated a Persistent Commitment to Clarity: The repeated mantra in emails and all-staff meetings was not merely a casual remark but a deliberate effort to establish clear expectations and to further reinforce his expectations.

Fostered a Shared Aspiration: Over time, employees started adopting the CEO's language and mindset. They integrated the phrase, "enjoy the day and be the best that you can be" into their own work, projects, and team interactions.

Applied Language in Problem-Solving: When challenges arose within projects or teams, leaders would mirror the CEO's language, asking questions such as, "How can we excel given this obstacle? How do we overcome it?" This indicated a cultural shift towards embracing the CEO's ethos and encouraging a proactive, solution-oriented approach.

This CEO's approach underscores the importance of deliberate communication in shaping organisational culture. By consistently reinforcing a clear message and cultivating a shared vision, the CEO effectively influenced behaviour and instilled a culture of accountability and excellence throughout the organisation.

He had a desired culture that he was leading the organisation towards. Do you?

It takes time and a considerable amount of effort to define your desired culture. I am all for co-creation of a desired culture and I have helped many an organisation to do so. In the next section, I share the secrets of what I do to support organisations to define their desired cultures.

First though, let's work on understanding the current culture as outlined in the previous chapter and in this diagram:

WHICH ONE IS YOUR WORKPLACE?

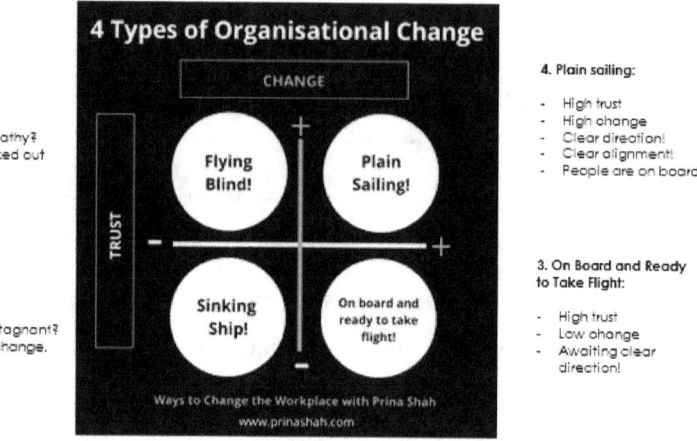

Consider where your organisation is placed...

Once everyone is on the same page about where the current culture is, we can then get into more detailed, and fun, work.

Activity: Defining Your Desired Culture Workshop

Here's a workshop outline to help you define your desired culture. To try and avoid your efforts resulting in a HIPPO void. HIPPO stands for, "highest paid person's opinion." Often, in hierarchical organisations, the views of the highest paid person in the room carry more weight than anybody else's. That's because we subconsciously endow highly paid people with a degree of authority and assume their ideas are superior simply because of their status. This can lead to a dangerous dynamic where innovative ideas and valuable input from others are overlooked or dismissed. The HIPPO effect stifles creativity and collaboration as team members may hesitate to voice their opinions or challenge the status quo, fearing it could be seen as disrespectful or unwise.

Imagine a boardroom where every decision is swayed by one voice, despite the diverse expertise and perspectives present. The company might miss out on groundbreaking solutions or fail to address critical issues effectively. The HIPPO effect can create a culture of complacency and conformity, where real progress is hindered by the echo of a single, dominant perspective.

Overcoming the HIPPO effect requires conscious effort and leadership commitment. It involves creating an environment where all voices are heard and valued, regardless of hierarchy.

Ideally, a seasoned facilitator should run this session to ensure neutrality and inclusivity and to avoid the HIPPO effect.

Workshop Steps in Summary:

1. **Introductions**: Start with introductions and the purpose of the session.
2. **Animal Exercise**: Ask participants what animal the organisation/team would be and why. This helps break the ice and encourages creativity.
3. **What is Our Current Culture?** Discuss where your workplace is using the quadrant above.
4. **Sails and Anchors**: Identify what drives the organisation/team forward (sails) and what holds it back (anchors). This helps celebrate strengths and address weaknesses.
5. **What's Missing?** Discuss what is missing based on the previous discussion. Address barriers and solutions.
6. **External Lens**: Consider external factors impacting the organisation and how the desired culture can meet these needs.

7. **Intermission**: Summarise the discussion and decide whether to continue or conclude the session.

8. **What We Stand For/Against**: Define clear statements of what the organisation stands for and against.

9. **Define Your Desired Culture**: Based on all the data gathered, you now have lots of data to determine and define your desired culture to aim for in the next 3-5 years.

Here is a detailed overview of the workshop.

Workshop Steps In The Form of A Run Sheet:

If you're the leader, ideally you will have a seasoned facilitator run this session for you so that you can take off your hierarchy hat and be involved in the conversation as a neutral party (and not as the HIPPO in the room).

If your umbrella organisational culture is crappy, this is one way you can create your own subculture. The onus is on you to lead the way with a head, a heart and a backbone.

Tip: Drop your judgements, expectations and have an open mind as it will enable creativity in yourself and in the other people involved in the session.

Section	Action	Why
Start	Introductions; and clarity on the purpose of today: to define our desired or aspirational culture. You can also share high level definitions of what organisational culture is.	Warm up the group dynamics, have decent introductions, and create inclusivity and interest.

Animals	If this organisation / division / team was an animal, what would it be and why? **Tip:** the facilitator should be seasoned to explore the deeper meanings of people's responses to capture the essence of the pros and cons of what has been said.	Beginning with such an activity throws people off guard and enables them to not only have fun and break their corporate shackles, but it also helps them to get their creative juices flowing.
Current Culture	Use the "which one is your workplace?" quadrant above to spark an honest conversation about your current culture.	Without knowing where our current culture is placed, we can't design or plan for a desired culture. We need to meet the organisation and people where they are at.
Ships	All ships have sails which take them forward and anchors which hold them in place. From your perspective of this organisation / division / team: • What are our sails? (The things that take us forward?) • What are our anchors? (The things that hold us down?) **Tip:** the facilitator should celebrate what is working (the sails) and further distil why. They should also delve into the things letting the team down (the anchors) to understand the root causes of the issues.	It is important to start with a positive and celebrate what is working (the sails). It is even more important to address the often-unsaid elephant in the room (the anchors); to understand the issues from a non-judgemental and non-punitive way, so that people's thoughts can be effectively understood, elaborated upon and captured.

What's missing?	Based on the above discussion, focus on the anchors responses to understand what is missing. Questions to ask: • Which anchors are weighing us down and what solutions do we have? • Why are the anchors so and how can we remove the barriers? What is it that needs to change?	This piece is the driving force of your desired culture and often goes unsaid in the right rooms but is the content of office gossip by the water cooler or on online chats. Why not address it now? This is the speak now or forever hold your peace part.
External lens	Look at the sails and anchors responses and take into account the external forces that impact our key corporate elements; such as our: • Board / shareholders • Customers • Our competitors • Products • Service delivery • The industry • The nature of our work • The nature of the landscape in which we work (political, social, economical, technological, resources) and how it is changing • Are we meeting those changing needs?	This is mixing traditional strategic planning elements with culture change principles. By enabling the right people to have a voice, it empowers them to define and determine the desired culture. It is best when all are involved as the buy-in for the change is already a need which has been met by the people involved.

	• If not, how do we need to BE to meet those needs (this is the start of defining your aspirational or desired culture. Use behavioural language here). **Tip:** A seasoned facilitator will enhance the conversation by encouraging people to respond in terms of behaviours and actions describing the way we wish to be; there is always room for improvement in any organisation, division or team.	
Intermission or session close prior to session 2	The facilitator needs to gather their thoughts to summarise all that has been discussed thus far. **Tip:** when I facilitate these sessions, I decide whether to call it to a close based on the energy, engagement and input of the room, or to continue on the process in the same session. If I pause between sessions, I will email the team a report laying out what has been discussed thus far and the next steps for session 2 as pre-work to warm them up.	Sometimes when I run these sessions, this is enough of a session to conclude with. It leaves people on a cliff-hanger and eager to move to the next stage.

What we stand for / what we stand against	Using the material gathered from the previous activities, the facilitator holds a discussion on: What do we therefore stand for? What do we stand against? **Tip:** these should be clear, concise statements in plain English. Post session: the facilitator to summarise the statements and work with the organisation, division or team to finalise the desired culture statements in relation to the things that we stand for and the things that we stand against, going forward. Then further work after the session is needed to have one voice of the desired culture. The final product could be a one-line clear statement. Supporting it could be the 'what we stand for' and 'what we stand against' statements.	This part essentially enables you to have a clear voice akin to the example I mentioned about the CEO who used to sign off as "enjoy the day and be the best that you can be." From my experience, there is a camaraderie and shared ownership created by such a collective session. Ideally if you are defining your desired culture at the organisational level, you will hold many of these sessions with employees at every level- not just at the top, and link them to your other workplace assets like your corporate strategic plans, your values, mission, etc. It paves the way for you to continue to use the information gathered from this session to articulate your desired or aspirational culture. It gives people a North Star.

You now have your desired culture articulated! This is how you begin to optimise your culture. You have a shared language to work off and to steer others.

Your action is to embed this into your workplace culture, into the way you communicate and the way the rest of the organisation behaves and moves forward.

People have used the outcomes of this session to:

- ☐ Add to their corporate strategic plans.
- ☐ Work on it on their awaydays.
- ☐ Add onto their internal documents.
- ☐ Include it to their vernacular as an executive team, as a divisional team, or as a team on the ground.
- ☐ To their performance and development processes.
- ☐ To their inductions.
- ☐ To their employee value propositions and so much more.

As new starters join they also need to learn the way. Your work is to determine how you embed your desired culture into your workplace, division or team.

Chapter Recap

You now understand how to define a desired culture, how to embed it into your work and how to embed it into your current culture. In this chapter, we've explored the process of defining your desired culture. By engaging in the workshop activities, you can articulate a clear vision for your organisation and create a shared understanding among your team.

Your Actions:

- ☐ Complete the Workshop to Define Your Desired Culture.
- ☐ Decide how you will embed this vision into your current culture.
- ☐ Prepare for the next chapter, where we'll discuss how to effectively convey your desired culture.

Notes:

CHAPTER 5

Effectively Conveying Your Desired Culture

> **Chapter Overview**
>
> Now that you have defined your desired culture, it's time to convey it effectively. This chapter will introduce the key marketing principles of the Know, Like and Trust concept that can help you communicate and embed your desired culture within your organisation. Trust is the cornerstone of many a meaningful outcome at work, and one which hasn't been discussed in the form of using marketing principles, until now… By the end of this chapter, you'll have practical strategies to ensure your desired culture is embraced by all.

The Power of Marketing Principles

Marketing principles can be incredibly effective in conveying and embedding your desired culture. By applying the principles of Know, Like, and Trust, you can build awareness, foster positive connections, and establish credibility within your organisation.

"Before a marketer can build trust, it must breed familiarity. But there's no familiarity without awareness. And awareness – [is] the science of letting people know you exist and getting them to understand your message." *Seth Godin, Permission Marketing: Turning Strangers Into Friends And Friends Into Customers.*

Now that you have defined your desired culture, the fun starts.

Your work now is to determine how you embed your desired culture into your workplace, division or team culture.

The secret sauce that I have found for many of my clients is through the application of marketing principles.

Yes, marketing principles.

I have worked with many organisations and teams in helping them to develop their culture and brand. By merging marketing principles with culture optimisation principles, you can transform the way your organisation operates and is perceived. The synergy of marketing principles and culture optimisation principles creates a powerful framework that goes beyond surface-level branding and culture change. It delves into the core of your organisation / division or team (its heartbeat,) aligning values, communication, and behaviours to create a cohesive and authentic brand identity.

Think about it: You've outlined your desired culture - a fresh approach to how things are done or how people behave. Just sticking to the basics won't spread it effectively throughout your organisation. Integrating it into your organisational fabric demands diligent effort. You must actively communicate and enlist others to embrace this new paradigm.

Otherwise, your efforts will be in vain, leaving your innovative approach neglected and causing frustration as your culture change remains elusive.

It is an exciting and a daunting phase, so let's work through a few marketing principles together.

Principles of Know, Like and Trust

The Know, Like, and Trust principles are widely attributed to Bob Burg, a speaker, author, and sales expert known for his book "*The Go-Giver.*" (It is well worth a listen on YouTube on 1.5 speed, if you like me, are a speed junkie). The principles have become a fundamental aspect of relationship-based marketing and business development.

These relationship-based marketing principles can be applied to communicating and showcasing your desired culture, and can also help you with activities such as:

- Developing your professional brand.
- Developing your organisational, divisional or team's professional brand.
- Showcasing your projects and accomplishments.
- Bringing people on the journey with you as a visionary leader.

Know, Like and Trust Marketing Principles Explained for Culture Change

Know: Building Awareness and Recognition

The Know phase focuses on establishing a robust presence in the minds of your target audience. This involves strategic efforts to increase brand visibility, enhance recognition, and ensure that your target demographic is aware of your products, services, or brand existence (or about your desired culture, in this case.)

Effective marketing strategies during this phase include brand storytelling, content marketing, social media engagement, and other initiatives aimed at putting your brand on the radar of potential customers (or employees in this case).

How are people going to <u>know</u> about your desired culture?

Like: Creating Positive Perceptions and Connections

Once your audience becomes acquainted with your brand (or about your desired culture in this case) the next step is to foster a positive connection with it. The Like phase is characterised by efforts to make your brand relatable, likeable, and aligned with the values and preferences of your audience. You are now tapping into people's hearts.

This involves showcasing your brand's personality, sharing authentic stories, and engaging in activities that resonate with your target demographic. Building a favourable perception contributes to the development of a genuine liking for your brand (or about your desired culture in this case).

How are people going to <u>like</u> your desired culture?

Trust: Establishing Credibility and Reliability

Trust is the bedrock of lasting relationships, good organisational cultures and an essential ingredient in high-performing teams. In the Trust phase, the focus shifts to building credibility and reliability.

This involves consistently delivering on promises, maintaining transparency, and demonstrating integrity in all business interactions.

If you are going to say you will do, let's say, a pulse survey every quarter for your desired culture, you best do it because all eyes are on you.

Customer testimonials, case studies, and a track record of reliability play pivotal roles in instilling confidence and trust in your brand (or about your desired culture in this case). This phase is crucial for cultivating long-term relationships, trust, and fostering customer loyalty (employee loyalty in this case).

This element of trust also refers to how you will consistently and equitably address those who work *against* your desired culture, this is the accountability piece which is often missing in many workplaces. How will you deal with those who do not comply with the new expectations?

How are people going to <u>trust</u> your desired culture?

In summary, the Know, Like, and Trust marketing principles form a sequential framework for cultivating meaningful relationships with your people. From initial awareness to creating positive connections and ultimately fostering trust, these principles provide a roadmap for building enduring relationships.

Case Study: McDonald's Know, Like, and Trust

To delve deeper, let's dissect a global brand example that we all may have come across. I have just seen my neighbour receive a food delivery, so forgive me for the junk food focus.

Caveat: I do not promote junk food. Learn to cook yourself, it is the best!

McDonald's is a global brand known for its consistent and reliable service. They have effectively applied the Know, Like, and Trust principles to build a strong brand identity. These principles can be adapted to communicate and embed your desired culture within your organisation.

- **Know:** McDonald's is a global fast-food chain recognised for its golden arches, iconic red and yellow colour scheme, and the famous "M" logo. The brand is synonymous with fast, convenient, and consistent food service.

- **Like:** McDonald's is liked for its diverse menu offerings, including the iconic Big Mac, Happy Meals, and signature fries. The brand's emphasis on affordability, convenience, and the familiarity of its products contributes to its likeability. Happy meals capture you from a young age.

- **Trust:** McDonald's has built trust through decades of delivering standardised and reliable fast food. The brand's commitment to quality control, safety standards, and efficient service contributes to consumer trust.

- **Slogan: "I'm Lovin' It":** This catchy and globally recognised slogan encapsulates the positive and enjoyable experience McDonald's aims to provide to its customers, making their meals a source of delight.

McDonald's has become a symbol of fast and accessible food, catering to diverse tastes across the globe. The brand's ability to adapt its menu to local preferences while maintaining a consistent global identity has contributed to its enduring popularity.

Imagine how McDonald's might apply the Know, Like and Trust principles to their culture.

To delve deeper into how McDonald's could drive cultural change using the principles of know, like, and trust, let's envision some engaging strategies:

Know: McDonald's could invest in comprehensive training programmes that go beyond teaching employees how to serve burgers and fries. They could highlight the brand's rich history, and its efforts towards sustainability. By ensuring that every employee understands and appreciates McDonald's background and future vision, the company can foster a deeper sense of pride and purpose among its workforces. This is the barbeque test as is referred to in Australia. What would you want your employees to say about your workplace at a barbeque on the weekend?

Like: Imagine McDonald's promoting a culture that celebrates diversity and inclusion, much like its diverse menu offerings. This could involve organising employee resource groups, hosting cultural events, and supporting community initiatives that resonate with employees from various backgrounds. By creating an inclusive environment where everyone feels valued, McDonald's can boost morale and strengthen employee loyalty.

Trust: McDonald's can build trust by emphasising transparency and accountability in its workplace practices. This might involve implementing open communication channels, establishing regular feedback loops, and ensuring fair treatment of all employees. Moreover, by investing in continuous training and development opportunities, McDonald's can demonstrate its commitment to supporting employee growth and well-being.

The questions for your consideration are:

- How will your desired culture stand the test of time for the next 3-5 years?
- How will you maintain the essence of your desired culture?

- What image do you wish to portray with your desired culture, and will it be playful, serious, or something else?
- What moments are your desired culture aspiring to build and what is your direct call to action for your desired culture?
- How will your desired culture appeal to your diverse workforce?

Apply Know, Like and Trust Principles to Your New Desired Culture

Reverting back to the CEO's line, which he still uses – "Enjoy the day and be the best that you can be." – People certainly *know* this person as their CEO.

Say you are working on developing your communication of your desired culture at the team level, your efforts will have to be heightened to ensure you and your work are *known*.

People *liked* this CEO for his directness and clear leadership. You knew where you stood. There was no grey area. (Not everyone will like you, the aim here is for the majority to develop a feeling of liking you).

As the CEO, people *trusted* him to lead the organisation in the right direction, which he did.

Now that you have defined your desired culture, it is time to work on communicating it. There are many ways that convey your desired culture to your organisation, division, team or colleagues.

Activity: Checklist for Deconstructing Know, Like, and Trust Principles

Use this checklist to communicate your desired culture effectively:

Know, Like, Trust	Checklist to Communicate Your Desired Culture (These are tasks you will have to repeat over and over and over again, as creating a new culture takes time and consistency).
Know: You can be the best-kept secret if you are unknown.	☐ Be clear on who you're talking to: Don't talk to "everybody". ☐ Curate the right content: Research, ask questions, listen, and delve further to ensure you create content that will touch the hearts and minds of your people. ☐ Use people power. Encourage sharing to a wider audience: This expands your message and helps more people get to know your desired culture. ☐ There is another marketing principle which the great Seth Godin talks about, it is to be remarkable. Remarkable is defined as being worthy of attention; striking, and it should be easily repeated. Your message must be remarkable in some way … sharing the new way, appealing, relatable, compelling etc. and must be repeatable. ☐ Ask the key influencers in your organisation to join forces with you: note your key influencers in the organisation may not be the ones in the traditional hierarchy. Consider the ones who create a buzz during water cooler chats or go wild and engage with the naysayers to be your advocates.

	☐	Create consistency: perhaps a specific page on your intranet to begin with. A flyer, consistent colours, consistent language, clear language. But please go beyond what I just stated – see what suits your organisational culture.
	☐	Get creative: it is not all about the written word. You can explore team development sessions, town hall all-staff meetings, webinars, your induction and onboarding, key celebrations in the workplace, internal podcasts, infographics, and video content to name a few. Consider your audience's needs.
	☐	Be visible: Putting a face to a name is everything.
Like: Without winning the hearts and minds of people, nothing will stick!	☐	Authenticity and your unique voice are essential elements.
	☐	Don't bore: it will detract from your message and not engage.
	☐	Practise what you preach: If you are going to state: "enjoy the day and be the best that you can be," you do it too, because all eyes are on you.
	☐	Initiate conversations: Invite your people to engage and interact with the new way. Invite comments, create a dialogue and ask questions.
	☐	Provide free resources in the form of posters, activities or training sessions people can attend. Create a buzz.
	☐	Be relevant: talk to the current pain points and why the new way is the right way. For example, we are currently understaffed and the holidays are looming. Even in this circumstance, you can state: "Enjoy the day and be the best that you can be."
	☐	Share content and promote ways to live your desired culture.
	☐	Deliver social proof: Or deliver quick wins and communicate and showcase those living your new desired culture, explain HOW they did so. Or even better, get them to explain.

Trust: The absence of trust is a dark force in an organisation, division or team.	☐ Keep promises: If you say you'll do something, do it. Breaking promises diminishes your credibility instantly. ☐ Consistency is queen, or king: "Enjoy the day and be the best that you can be," wasn't only at the end of the CEO's emails. It was in his vernacular, in his behaviour and in everything he embodied. ☐ Use case studies: Real-world examples (and proof) of the new way enables others to follow and learn. ☐ Keep it simple: People have an inbuilt BS detector and know when you are being disingenuous. ☐ Also be sure to reach the non-English speakers with clear language (there are many of us out there). ☐ If you mess up, fess up: Apologise when you need to. You're not always going to get it right. Your people will hold you in much higher regard than attempting to conceal it unsuccessfully. (You and I have many stories of those who have tried to conceal the truth, we know how that ends). ☐ Offer consistent behavioural prompts: "Enjoy the day and be the best that you can be," isn't a generic statement, it is a way to be. It is a clear direction for me to check in on myself.

Chapter Recap

In this chapter, we've explored how to effectively convey your desired culture using marketing principles. By applying the Know, Like, and Trust principles, you can build awareness, foster positive connections, and establish credibility within your organisation.

Your Actions:

- ☐ Complete the Checklist for Deconstructing Know, Like, and Trust Principles.
- ☐ Implement these strategies to communicate your desired culture.
- ☐ Prepare for the next chapter, where we'll discuss how to build a solid team.

Notes:

CHAPTER 6
Building a Solid Team

> **Chapter Overview**
>
> A meaningful legacy cannot be created alone. This chapter focuses on building a solid team that supports and shares your vision. We'll explore strategies to foster teamwork, address burnout, and create a cohesive, high-performing team.

The Importance of Teamwork

Teamwork is essential in creating a meaningful legacy. A strong team can amplify your efforts and help sustain the desired culture. However, building such a team requires intentional effort and strategic planning.

For any meaningful work which leads to creating a legacy, you need to have a high-performing team surrounding you. You simply cannot do it alone.

I have seen far too many people managers trying to run a one-person show at work. It works initially and they receive accolades based on their successes, they are put on great projects or touted as an employee with "high potential," or they are on the watch list of performers to be retained in the organisation.

A past manager of mine fell into this category. They were the head of People and Culture.

A good operator.

They prioritised their career ambitions and excelled, earning recognition and ultimately winning a prestigious HR Manager of the Year award. It was a fantastic accolade. One that the whole team was proud of.

Only the CEO, my colleague and I were invited to the award ceremony as heads of our respective areas, excluding the rest of the team.

The rest of the team started to show signs of disengagement and dissatisfaction. People were happy for the new award of their leader but felt left out. They wanted to join the celebration.

This situation underscores the importance of balancing one's personal career aspirations with effective leadership and team management.

I will focus on team management in this chapter (*and on how you can lead with a head, heart and backbone in the next chapter. These are things that every people manager should have been taught but weren't*). If you are not a direct team leader, you can still apply the below to your team as a peer. You are a leader bringing about positive change in your own right in this perspective.

Case Study: The Burnout Checklist

In many organisations, I have noticed high levels of burnout. Working alone as a people manager is unsustainable in the long term. To create a meaningful culture that leaves a legacy, you need to bring your people along and build a solid team.

I've seen many leaders fall into a slow-motion career crash. Burnout doesn't happen overnight; it creeps up on you. Here are some signs that burnout may be on the horizon. See if you relate to any:

- ☐ Your once-manageable to-do list now feels overwhelming.
- ☐ You frequently jump between maker mode (the doing) and manager mode (leading).
- ☐ Your team isn't effectively taking on extra work (possibly due to lack of delegation, disengagement, or poor communication).
- ☐ You find it difficult to focus on the bigger picture and long-term goals.
- ☐ You're acting as a martyr, with a busy diary and the mindset of "No one else can get it right, so I may as well take it on myself."
- ☐ You feel overwhelmed and stressed, unable to find time for self-care or to recharge.
- ☐ You start experiencing physical symptoms like headaches, fatigue, digestive issues, or insomnia – your body's way of signalling that it needs rest.

Burnout doesn't just affect you; it jeopardises your ability to make work meaningful and create a lasting legacy so you must check yourself, before you wreck yourself. Building a strong team and cultivating a supportive culture is essential. By doing so, you ensure your efforts are sustained and amplified, enabling you to focus on what truly matters – creating a culture makes work meaningful.

A good team culture will result in the opposite of a burnout culture:

Increased Productivity: A supportive team culture encourages collaboration and delegation, allowing tasks to be shared effectively, reducing individual burdens, and boosting overall productivity.

Enhanced Engagement: When employees feel valued and empowered within a positive team culture, they become more engaged and motivated to contribute creatively and proactively to achieve common goals.

Improved Communication: A strong team culture fosters open communication, where ideas flow freely, concerns are addressed constructively, and feedback is welcomed, leading to better problem-solving and decision-making.

Better Work-Life Integration: A supportive team culture recognises the importance of work-life integration, encouraging flexible working arrangements and promoting living well. This helps prevent burnout and enhances overall job satisfaction.

Long-Term Focus: With a cohesive team culture, individuals can focus more on the bigger picture and long-term goals, as responsibilities are shared, and trust is established among team members.

Resilience to Challenges: A strong team culture builds resilience, enabling teams to navigate challenges together effectively, learn from setbacks, and adapt to changing circumstances.

By nurturing a positive team culture, leaders can mitigate the risk of burnout, foster a collaborative and resilient workforce, and drive sustained success in the face of evolving challenges. This approach not only supports individual well-being but also strengthens the overall performance and cohesion of the organisation.

It is not only about only you leaving a legacy, ideally, you are creating a great team which will leave a legacy.

I have been coaching a high-ranking leader in the upper echelons. She is fabulous. Her accolades have surpassed her and most people's expectations.

When we first began our coaching relationship, she told me she's been very "lucky" in her career.

She had been placed, or tapped on the shoulder, to be put into the best jobs after achieving success for many organisations.

Why did she want to work with me? She is now at a stage where she has realised that at times she has been *dragged* into her career, *rather than taking the reins* and driving her career.

This was a significant aha moment.

She realised that her and the team work as highly effective lone rangers. They are not a team... yet.

We have worked together on developing not only her, but now I am also upskilling her team to ensure that she has the best support and is paving the right way forward.

The team themselves are superstars in their own right.

They too are lone rangers who have achieved significant global career successes.

The issue is that the whole team operates as individuals rather than a unit when it comes to certain aspects of the way they work.

Activity: How to Identify Lone Ranger (Silo) Teams

In the fast-paced world of work, Lone Ranger Team syndrome (or silo working) can silently seep into a team's dynamics, hindering collective success.

See if the below applies to your situation by doing a self-assessment, marking an 'x' in the appropriate place on the scale below.

> **Here are eight practical and relatable signs of Lone Ranger or silo behaviour within a team and why it's detrimental to the greater good. Consider where your team is placed.**
>
> **1. Silos of Excellence:** Team members excel individually but struggle to integrate their strengths as a collective. This creates isolated pockets of brilliance, limiting the synergies that come from collaborative efforts.
>
> **Scale: How does your team relate? (Place an 'x' on where your team is).**
>
> <-->
>
> **Not at all like this**   **Very much like this**
>
> **2. Communication Breakdowns:** Due to the fast-paced solo way in which they work, Lone Rangers often fail to communicate effectively, withholding critical information or insights. This lack of shared communication impedes the flow of ideas and prevents the team from functioning cohesively as a collective.
>
> **Scale: How does your team relate? (Place an 'x' on where your team is).**
>
> <-->
>
> **Not at all like this**   **Very much like this**

3. Inefficient Resource Allocation: When team members operate in isolation, there's a risk of duplicated efforts and misallocation of resources. A unified team can better coordinate tasks and allocate resources judiciously to maximise time and efficiency.

Scale: How does your team relate? (Place an 'x' on where your team is).

<-->

Not at all like this   **Very much like this**

4. Overloaded Team Leader: The team leader, acting as a lone wolf, may shoulder an overwhelming amount of responsibility. This can lead to burnout and negatively impact their own work.

Scale: How does your team relate? (Place an 'x' on where your team is).

<-->

Not at all like this   **Very much like this**

5. Limited Learning and Development: Lone Rangers may resist sharing knowledge or mentoring others, due to the simple fact that it may not have been a consideration for them, thus hindering the growth of team members. A collaborative environment fosters continuous learning, ensuring that the team evolves and learns together.

Scale: How does your team relate? (Place an 'x' on where your team is).

<-->

Not at all like this   **Very much like this**

6. Stifled Innovation: Lone Ranger teams may struggle to innovate as individual perspectives dominate. A lack of diverse input hinders creative problem-solving, limiting the team's ability to adapt to challenges and seize new opportunities.

Scale: How does your team relate? (Place an 'x' on where your team is).

<-->

Not at all like this   **Very much like this**

7. Risk of Talent Attrition: Team members operating in isolation might feel undervalued or disconnected. This results in an extended reliance on the head of the team as their only go-to person, or it increases the risk of talented individuals seeking opportunities elsewhere, ultimately weakening the overall team structure.

Scale: How does your team relate? (Place an 'x' on where your team is).

<-->

Not at all like this   **Very much like this**

8. Erosion of Team Morale: The absence of a unified team spirit can lead to diminished morale. Team members may feel isolated, demotivated, and disengaged, impacting their overall job satisfaction, team culture and commitment to shared goals.

Scale: How does your team relate? (Place an 'x' on where your team is).

<-->

Not at all like this   **Very much like this**

Recognising these signs is the first step toward building a strong, cohesive team that can collectively achieve lasting success. Breaking free from the Lone Ranger mindset requires intentional efforts to foster collaboration, open communication, and a shared sense of purpose.

How to Unify Your Team

After reflecting on the list, you may have identified the need to unify your team.

You may have been operating in a silo manner for a while, and now things need to change.

I have supported many teams to unify and to excel whether they are Lone Ranger teams or teams of a different, high performing or toxic sort. Building a solid team and unifying your people takes time and effort from all involved.

To begin with and to ensure people get to change their behaviour, it is essential that the individual team members understand where each other are at.

Nothing changes if nothing changes is a line you may have heard. In this context, by acknowledging that meaningful change requires proactive effort and a willingness to question and challenge the status quo and break from the familiar, you are making headway in forging a new and ideally better path.

Even if your team are not Lone Rangers per se, there still may be something missing in the way you connect and work with each other.

I guarantee you will not have understood them in the manner that I am going to show you…

Activity: Reflect on Your Team's Achievements

Take time to reflect on your team's achievements. Celebrate successes and identify areas for improvement. Use the following questions to guide your reflection:

- What have we achieved together?
- What challenges have we overcome?
- How can we improve our teamwork?

The below activity is one of many I use to unite a team. It is one of my preferred activities when working with a team to identify their pleasures, sorrows, dynamics and structures.

The activity of exploring and sharing answers to the quadrant-based questions in a team development session (or team optimisation, as I call it) holds significant importance in your mission to understand the current state and then to build a solid team.

Lone ranger teams use "I" more than "We."

Whether you are a Lone Ranger team, or a team of a different sort, it is crucial to tap into that individual thinking as it enables each person to articulate where they are at.

Below is an activity that you can conduct in a team development or team strategy session.

Before your session, ask each individual on the team to consider their answers to this grid and bring their answers to share. By prompting this individual preparation, you stop groupthink and you will ideally receive more genuine responses.

These questions can be asked at the end of a project, at the end of the year, or at any milestone where you wish to gain an understanding of the current state of your individual team members:

- In the bottom left quadrant: what felt like low achievement and low pride for you? (Failed this!)
- In the top left quadrant: what felt like high achievement and low pride for you? (Did this!)
- In the bottom right quadrant: what felt like high pride, but low achievement for you? (Glad it happened!)
- In the top right quadrant: What felt like high achievement and high pride for you? (Nailed this!)

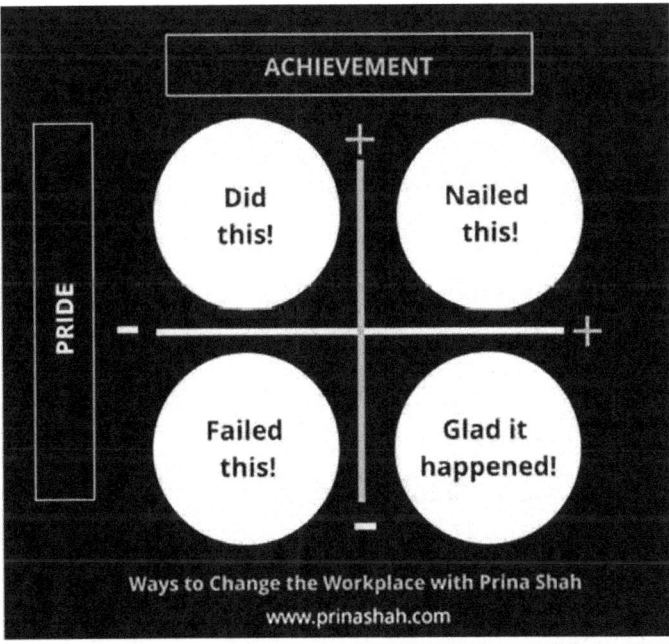

> **By asking these questions, or using a seasoned facilitator to do so, this activity will help you to:**
>
> - Uncover what individuals think went well and not so well.
> - Have an open discussion about the past year through a fresh lens.
> - Plan for the next year, milestone or project.
> - Bonus: as a leader, you'll learn the pain points of your team and know how to further support and unify them! This is the start of unifying your team!

I facilitated the above activity for the Lone Ranger team that I wrote about earlier. This activity resulted in a shared sense of understanding of each other as peers. It resulted in peers connecting on a deeper level and in the session, people offered each other help in the form of, "I didn't know you were facing that too; we should chat offline to see how we can address the issues together." It resulted in the team celebrating the successes of their peers that they wouldn't have known of otherwise. It resulted in people being vulnerable in sharing what they felt they failed at, and it enabled a longer-term view on what needed to be done to enable people to better achieve their goals. (We discussed system issues, things holding them back, and how to enable better ways of working). The leader gained so much information from it that she is working one on one with each team member to continue the conversation on how to support them.

This activity has enabled the leader to support herself and the team members to work their way through the legacy and achievement paradox; to progress from "Legacy Dreamers" to "Legacy Believers," "Legacy Feeders," and ultimately, to "Legacy Leaders."

An Impactful Approach to Building a Solid Team:

This is an impactful approach to building a solid team as this activity enables the whole team to self-reflect in their own manner to begin with as individuals. It stops groupthink and peer pressure as the team are required to come prepared with answers to the activity prior to the session. It goes beyond a traditional strengths, weaknesses, opportunities and threats (SWOT) activity as it enables individuals to truly self-reflect using the notion of pride in their considerations. How often is it that we are asked what we are proud of at work? Taking this approach enables better insights into each team member. It has also resulted in deeper connections between team members when I have facilitated this activity.

Benefits of the Activity for the Team:

Individual Reflection and Awareness: The activity prompts team members to reflect on their experiences and categorise them into specific quadrants. This introspection encourages self-awareness and a deeper understanding of personal achievements and challenges.

Open Discussion and Transparency: By sharing their reflections within the team, individuals contribute to a transparent and open discussion. This process breaks down communication barriers and fosters an environment where team members feel comfortable expressing both successes and areas that need improvement.

> **Tip:** For best results, it is important that the leader also gets involved and hands over the reins to a trusted facilitator to run this activity. Without the leader getting involved, no one else will feel it worthwhile and they will feel as if they are being monitored. That is counterproductive to what you are trying to achieve.

A Reflection with a Fresh Vulnerable Perspective: The activity provides a unique, vulnerable and fresh lens through which team members can revisit their achievements and results. It allows them to evaluate their experiences not only in terms of achievements but also in relation to pride, creating a holistic view of their professional journey. It taps into their hearts as well as minds.

Strategic Planning for the Future: As individuals share their reflections, the team gains insights into what worked well and what didn't. This collective understanding becomes a foundation for future strategic planning, enabling the team to collectively identify areas for improvement and set meaningful goals going forward. The leader will also become less burdened in time.

Enhanced Team Cohesion: Through the process of sharing successes, challenges, and aspirations, team members develop a sense of trust, affinity, and a shared experience. This shared understanding forms the basis for enhanced cohesion, as team members realise that they are part of a collective journey with common goals and common issues. They will start to rely more on each other and less on the leader in time.

Benefits of the Activity for the Leader:

Insight into Team Dynamics

For leaders, the activity acts as a starting point for unifying the team. It serves as a valuable tool for gaining insights into the team's pain points and triumphs. Understanding individual perspectives helps leaders tailor their support, addressing specific needs and challenges. This knowledge is fundamental to effective leadership and team unification.

By openly discussing achievements and challenges, the team lays the groundwork for a collaborative and supportive environment. This shared understanding becomes the foundation upon which team unity can be nurtured and strengthened.

In essence, the pre-session activity with the quadrant-based questions is a powerful tool that goes beyond a mere reflection exercise. It serves as a catalyst for team unity by fostering individual awareness, open communication, strategic planning, and deep leadership insights. This shared experience becomes the cornerstone for a cohesive, united and a solid high-performing team. It becomes a foundation for future team work going forward.

After all, for any meaningful work which leads to creating a legacy, you need to have a high-performing and engaged team surrounding you. This is your first step to building a solid team.

Chapter Recap

In this chapter, we've discussed the importance of building a solid, united team and strategies to foster teamwork and address burnout. You will now have a guide on how to unite silo or Lone Ranger teams using the activity to enable you to tap into the individual's core needs and motivations. By reflecting on your team's achievements and continuously striving for improvement, you can create a supportive and high-performing team which will make your work life far more meaningful.

Your Actions:

- ☐ Reflect on your team's achievements by conducting the activity.
- ☐ Score your team on Lone Ranger or silo behaviour.
- ☐ Implement strategies to foster teamwork and address burnout.
- ☐ Determine the way forward from what you have learned from the activities.
- ☐ Prepare for the next chapter, where we'll discuss building alliances for your professional brand.

Notes:

CHAPTER 7
Building Alliances

> **Chapter Overview**
>
> No leader is an island. Building strong alliances is essential for creating a meaningful legacy. This chapter focuses on the importance of professional networks and provides practical strategies for building and maintaining these alliances.

The Power of Alliances

Strong professional networks can provide support, resources, and opportunities for growth. Building alliances with the right people can help you achieve your goals and create a lasting impact.

Building the right alliance is something that I learned early on as a sociology and social psychology student at university. In this chapter, I share a personal story of how I learned to build an alliance in those days, plus a practical guide on creating eight important alliances for yourself.

Case Study: You'll Never Walk Alone

Early in my university days, I learned the importance of having the right alliances. I was a diligent student, focused on my grades, but I was missing a key element: the support of others.

My university boyfriend was a die-hard Liverpool Football Club fan. Football bored me to tears, but his passion intrigued me. He explained that his loyalty to Liverpool stemmed from their anthem, "You'll Never Walk Alone." This song wasn't just a tune; it was a mantra that fostered a sense of unity and collective support among the fans.

This concept fascinated me. How could a song create such a powerful, collective identity? It wasn't just about the music; it was about what the song represented – a promise that you're never alone, no matter what. This notion aligns perfectly with the Know, Like, and Trust principles in marketing.

Know: The song made Liverpool fans feel known and understood. It spoke to their experiences and emotions, creating an immediate connection.

Like: It built a community where fans were part of something bigger than themselves, fostering camaraderie and mutual support.

Trust: The consistent message of the song built trust. Fans knew that in good times and bad, they had a community that stood by them.

By building these alliances, Liverpool FC fostered a culture of loyalty and support. This same principle applies to your professional life. To create a meaningful culture and leave a legacy, you need to build strong alliances based on these principles.

I was studying for a bachelor of science in sociology and social psychology and this was right up my alley. What was this phenomenon that brought about a collective consciousness, this shared social solidarity of a group of people whom I would snobbishly (usually) term as yobs, football hooligans or in good Australian vernacular; hoons? The song "You'll Never Walk Alone" enabled fans to connect with each other at another level *and* it set a behavioural expectation.

This song united Liverpool FC fans. It was something I had never seen before. It certainly has the Know, Like and Trust marketing principles which talks to its longevity. Look up the lyrics if you are interested.

Choosing Not to Walk Alone

So, how can you apply this to your own career?

What does it mean for you to never walk alone in the career sense?

Since hearing the song in my late teens at university, I decided to take it on as meaning that I needed to expand my network and never walk alone.

My first step was to reach out to a great lecturer to ask him to be my mentor for my thesis.

I have valued mentorship since then and I have expanded the meaning of it as my career has evolved because I understood that not one person could fit the bill for all of my career needs.

Have you considered what career needs you have, and therefore what *kinds* of people you need around you? Based on your answer to that loaded question, you will be able to determine how you can find the right person or people to support you so that you don't have to walk alone.

Over the last 20+ years, I have come across this through coaching clients, facilitating mentoring programs and consulting executives on developing their professional brand. There are eight people I believe add the most value to your network, in turn helping you scale your full potential. These are people who may currently be in your life, or maybe they're yet to enter your life. Many people do not consider their network in this manner and once you do, you will see the reciprocal benefits of such alliances.

Who are these eight people?

The Inspirational Guide This person keeps you energised and motivated – they have a positive outlook on life and always see the glass as half full. You go to them when you need inspiration and encouragement.

The Strategic Inquirer This person is inquisitive and does not take anything at face value. They will probe, and ask you clear, insightful and sometimes uncomfortable questions. They force you to think beyond the superficial level.

The Pragmatic Adviser This person says it like it is, but with compassion. They have your best interests at heart but don't beat around the bush. They care about you and want to make sure that you do not get in your own way with blind spots or excuses.

The Leadership Sherpa This person provides strategies to help you show up as the self-actualised version of your current self. They provide tools and ideas to help you navigate through situations and always push for the best outcome. They enable you to be forward thinking. People often pay for a coach; someone they have a rapport with and who they have researched.

The Empathetic Perspective This person makes us feel heard and supported. Their role is there to hear you and guide you to find your own solutions and perspectives.

The Accountability Partner This person holds you accountable and does not accept excuses. They will stay on your back until you beat your personal best. They do not accept a 50% effort - they want you to give it all!

The Catalyst for Growth This person pushes you out of your comfort zone. While the strategic inquirer asks uncomfortable questions, this person pushes you into uncomfortable situations for your personal growth – they make us face our fears.

The Networking Maestro This is the person who has a massive tribe. They walk into a room of strangers and walk out with allies. They have a vast network of people, and they can provide you with connections and resources.

Let's delve deeper to consider how you can ensure you never walk alone.

Activity: Self-Assessment of Professional Alliances

Reflect on the following questions to assess your professional network:

- Who are the key people in my professional network?
- How do these relationships support my goals?
- Where can I build new alliances?
- How can I strengthen existing relationships?

I have outlined eight people that you need in your network to bring out the best from you. No one person will be able to tick all of the boxes, though there may be some people in your network who cover more than one set of qualities.

Below are descriptions of the eight people you need and instructions on how they can assist you.

- ☐ If conducting the activity as an individual, open your contact list and see who fits.

Make Work Meaningful

- ☐ If conducting the activity as a team, consider who will be best to support your collective efforts.
- ☐ Identify and reach out to at least three people. This activity can be considered as an individual or as a team.

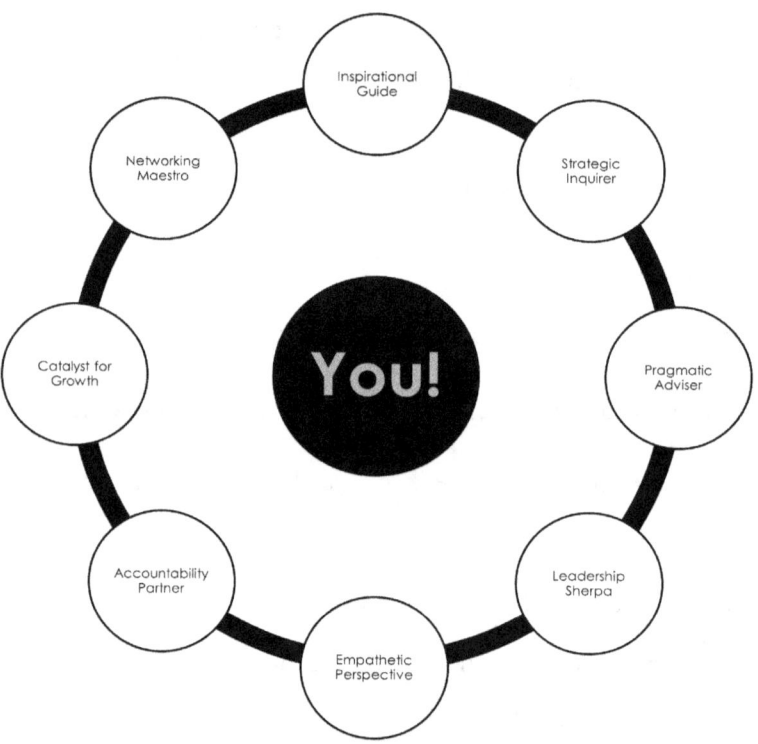

The Inspirational Guide

- ☐ Within your network, identify an individual who consistently provides motivation and energy.
- ☐ This person maintains an optimistic outlook on professional challenges and serves as a source of inspiration and encouragement.

Name of person to contact:

The Strategic Inquirer
☐ Cultivate a connection with someone who challenges your leadership thinking through insightful and probing questions. ☐ This individual encourages you to delve beyond surface-level considerations, fostering a strategic mindset.
Name of person to contact:

The Pragmatic Adviser
☐ Seek out a confidant who offers honest feedback with a compassionate approach. ☐ This person is invested in your success, ensuring you navigate challenges with clarity and without succumbing to blind spots.
Name of person to contact:

The Leadership Sherpa
☐ Establish a mentorship or formal paid coaching relationship with, ideally, a qualified coach who provides actionable strategies for your self-actualization. ☐ This coach or mentor equips you with tools and insights to navigate complex leadership scenarios, consistently pushing you for optimal outcomes.
Name of person to contact:

The Empathetic Perspective
☐ Ensure you have a trusted ally in your network who excels in active listening and providing empathetic support. ☐ This person aids in finding your own solutions and perspectives, crucial during pivotal leadership moments.
Name of person to contact:

The Accountability Partner
☐ Identify an individual who holds you accountable, refusing to accept excuses.
☐ This accountability partner motivates you to take a detour from the shiny object syndrome we often succumb to, to surpass your personal bests by driving continuous improvement.
Name of person to contact:

The Catalyst for Growth
☐ Cultivate a relationship with someone who actively pushes you beyond your comfort zone.
☐ This individual stimulates personal and professional growth by encouraging you to face and conquer fears and limitations.
Name of person to contact:

The Networking Maestro
☐ Connect with an individual possessing a vast network, capable of turning strangers into allies effortlessly.
☐ Learn the art of relationship building and maintaining skills from this person.
☐ Leverage this person's extensive connections for strategic alliances and access to valuable resources. Note: there's giving and taking. Remember the rule of reciprocity. *Don't be a constant taker.*
Name of person to contact:

This could well be the game changer you need to help you to make work meaningful.

Identifying and connecting with these people will not only help you build an expansive network but challenge the unconscious parameters of your own ways of thinking. As a result of these collaborative networks, I've seen many clients and peers achieve more frequent, and more valuable and rewarding, personal and professional triumphs after applying this activity.

Caveat – go in with the abundance mindset of <u>giving</u> and not taking, in all of the above relationships. It is a two-way street.

Your networks are important. Regular and genuine attention to these relationships will contribute to your sustained success as you cannot do it alone. Many leaders I support don't have a decent network of this sort, especially the higher they climb up the corporate ladder. They tend to get more and more lonely in the work sense.

The higher one climbs up through the corporate ranks, the fewer trusted people in one's network there tend to be. This is a sign to watch out for in the course of your career, wherever you are in the hierarchy. Relationships are nurturing as you have no doubt seen from the people who have supported you in your career.

It is not a one-way street with relationships. Giving back to give forward is a mindset to develop as it will enable richer relationships and remind you of the fact that you cannot do this work solo.

You cannot do it alone. Creating a culture that leaves a legacy needs to be a collective and generous effort.

With that in mind, it is imperative for you to consider who you would like to be there for too. To think beyond yourself.

Throughout my career I have either mentored people or given back in the form of pro bono coaching. With this pass-it-on mentality I am able to assist someone else who is now where I once was. This ensures that I give back; it's part of my legacy.

Side Note: Who Do You Advocate For? How To Be an Ally

It's not all about you. Be an ally…

You can impact others in direct ways, and this is for your consideration. As you start to develop not only yourself, your team and your division, what are you doing to enable others who don't have a voice to shine?

In the corporate world, I have often noticed a lack of camaraderie or fellowship when it comes to supporting people who are underrepresented.

I was born in Kenya and brought up in the United Kingdom. I am of Indian origin (Gujarati,) and now am an Australian citizen. I am female and was always being touted as "talent" or as a "high performer" when I was in the corporate world. I however had no one advocating for me at work. It felt lonely and I got fed up of being labelled as "the only one". It felt very solitary. I felt like I was walking alone even though I was labelled as "one to watch". While I met the diversity targets of the organisations that I served and a few organisations used me as their token brown or ethnic poster child, they didn't do much to reciprocate for me.

How to Be an Ally

So, to apply the "You'll never walk alone" philosophy to the people in your workplace who need that extra advocacy, what will you do?

It is not only for CEOs and leaders to advocate for others, we can also all do so.

Here are a few novel ideas to get you thinking beyond traditional measures. Consider the below for those who are underrepresented at your workplace.

Reflective Activity: Novel Ideas for Building Inclusive Networks and Advocacy

Consider how you need to lift your game to support others to shine. You are able to ensure that others also don't walk alone using these ideas. Decide on what you can implement.

Reverse Mentorship Programs:

Establish programs where diverse employees mentor senior leaders, providing insights into emerging trends, technology, and diverse perspectives. This innovative approach can break hierarchical barriers, build connections and enrich the culture of your organisation. It will also be a circuit breaker for stale people at the top who need a shot of reality.

Advocacy Pods:

Form small advocacy groups or "pods" where members actively support each other's professional growth. Encourage these pods to include diverse individuals, ensuring mutual advocacy within the group.

Leadership Shadowing Experiences:

Facilitate shadowing opportunities where leaders can spend a day immersed in the roles of underrepresented employees. This hands-on experience fosters empathy, understanding, and opens avenues for meaningful advocacy.

Inclusive Networking Platforms:

Create platforms dedicated to fostering diversity and inclusion within your organisation. These platforms can serve as a space for sharing success stories, challenges, and opportunities, fostering a sense of belonging and understanding.

Advocacy or Allyship Training Workshops:

Conduct workshops that train leaders on effective advocacy or ally techniques. Equip them with the skills to champion the causes of underrepresented individuals, ensuring they have vocal supporters in crucial discussions.

Collaborative Mentorship Circles:

Encourage the formation of mentorship circles where individuals from different backgrounds come together to share insights and experiences. This collaborative approach provides a supportive network for everyone involved and creates a space to share stories and learn from one another.

Advocacy Sprints:

Implement short-term advocacy initiatives, or "sprints," where leaders actively support the career goals of underrepresented individuals. This focused approach ensures that advocacy efforts are impactful, focused and time-bound.

Interactive Inclusion Forums:

Host regular forums or town hall meetings focused on inclusion. Use these platforms to discuss challenges faced by underrepresented groups and collaboratively brainstorm solutions, fostering a sense of shared responsibility.

Remember, these ideas aim not only to build a network, but to create a culture of advocacy and support.

By implementing these (or your own) novel approaches, you contribute to a workplace where everyone feels heard, supported, and empowered to thrive and where no one ideally walks alone.

Why not try something new at your workplace? It is not about walking alone. It is about learning from others and raising those who do not have a voice.

Chapter Recap

In this chapter, we've discussed the importance of building alliances and strategies for maintaining strong professional networks. By assessing and strengthening your professional relationships, you can create a supportive network that helps you achieve your legacy goal in order to make work meaningful.

Your Actions:

- ☐ Conduct the Self-Assessment of Professional Alliances.
    - ☐ Decide on the action you need to take and reach out to at least three of those people to begin with – make it happen.
    - ☐ Determine how often you will meet.
    - ☐ Determine how you will self-reflect after the meetings.
    - ☐ Determine how you intend to reciprocate to build and strengthen your professional network.
- ☐ Consider who you will be an ally for and how with the ideas provided.
- ☐ Prepare for the next chapter, where we'll explore how to lead with head, heart, and backbone.

Notes:

CHAPTER 8

Leading with Head, Heart, and Backbone

> **Chapter Overview**
>
> Balanced leadership is crucial for creating a meaningful legacy. It is now time to step up and focus on you and how you are leading. I believe that everyone is a leader, not only those with an appointed title. In this chapter you will learn concepts of how to lead with the head (using your discernment), the heart (compassion) and with backbone (grit). These are essential skills for all to develop. By the end of this chapter, you'll have practical strategies to ensure your leadership is balanced and effective.

The Balance of Leadership

Leading with head, heart, and backbone means balancing logic, empathy, and courage. This balanced approach ensures that your decisions are well-rounded and considerate of both organisational goals and individual needs.

You are now on the path to building a solid team. Hoorah.

At this point you might also begin to mentally burden yourself as it has unlocked a new version of the team and a new version of yourself. I refer to this as when we reach new levels, we also face new devils.

Case Study: New Levels, New Devils

At this juncture, you might start to feel a sense of trepidation, as it signifies a transformation within the team and within yourself. Establishing a robust team can evoke a mix of excitement and difficulty. The expression "new levels, new devils" encapsulates this sentiment precisely. It acknowledges that with every step forward, there are new challenges to overcome.

In this phase, it's crucial to recognise that challenges are inherent to progress.

Your role now involves navigating these new challenges, fostering a resilient team culture, and adapting your leadership style to meet the evolving needs of the team.

Embrace the discomfort (your new devils) as a sign of growth and use it as an opportunity to refine your leadership skills.

Remember, as you build a solid team, you're not just shaping the team's future, but also your own.

Embracing this transformation means not only evolving the team but also evolving yourself as a leader to lead with a head, heart and a backbone.

When I studied for my diploma of professional coaching, my teacher dropped the term "head, heart and backbone" a few times when we were doing role plays as part of my certification.

Leading with a head, heart and backbone is what I will now elaborate upon.

I was a people manager, the Head of People and Culture for one of the largest not-for-profits in Western Australia at the time.

I was receiving many accolades for my work.

My situation had me hitting new levels and many new devils. By this I mean more was expected of me and I realised that imposter syndrome had surfaced. I don't like the term imposter syndrome; I prefer to refer to it as a crisis of confidence, which is exactly what happened. Your devils may take a different form.

The organisation was growing at a rapid speed; doing more and expanding our service range.

My team was growing at a rapid speed and expected to do more in the new, fast-evolving landscape.

I started to stress myself out because I could not keep up.

I knew that I had to level up my leadership game. But how?

More than ever, faced with these new challenges and responsibilities, I needed to lead with a head, heart and a backbone.

How To Lead with Head, Heart, and Backbone

The "**head**" signifies the intellectual aspect of leadership, making strategic decisions, and navigating complexities with a clear and thoughtful mind. As the Head of People and Culture, my strategic thinking and decision-making were instrumental in supporting the people's needs, my team's needs and the organisation's growth.

In the people and culture role, being the "head" wasn't about fancy strategies and complex decisions—it was more like being the captain of a team and steering my people in the right direction. It often meant thinking on my feet and making choices that not only benefited the organisation but also considered the needs of each team member. Imagine balancing different priorities, like making sure people were growing professionally, the team was working well together, and the company was moving forward. It's like putting together a puzzle where every piece matters. Juggling is another way to put it. So, being in the "head" space wasn't about being a genius in front of the board; it was about making real, everyday decisions that helped (ideally) *everyone* to grow effectively together.

The "**heart**" embodies the emotional intelligence and empathy needed to connect with my team, stakeholders and the executive on a richer level. Understanding, appreciating, and when necessary, addressing these differing concerns, aspirations, and emotions became even more critical for our collective growth, as people and as an organisation. It was an exciting, scary and stressful period.

In the world of the "heart" space, it was like stepping into the emotional arena of the workplace. As the Head of People and Culture, it wasn't just about policies and procedures; it was about connecting with individuals on a human level. Picture this: it's not just about knowing someone's job title; it's about understanding what makes them tick, what keeps them up at night, and what dreams they're chasing. (And remembering as much as I possibly could about the 1500+ employees that I was serving). This emotional intelligence wasn't just reserved for the team; it extended to my clients (all employees), my stakeholders and the bigwigs in the executive suite. It felt a bit like being the team's emotional translator - navigating through excitement, fears, and stresses, while managing my own funk too. These were fun times which I learned a lot from.

The "**backbone**" represents the courage and resilience required to make tough decisions, stand firm in my convictions, and lead with integrity. As challenges arose, having the backbone to navigate uncertainties and maintain a strong leadership presence became a defining factor in the way I and my team operated.

The "backbone" is the part that felt like being the sturdy pillar holding everything up. As challenges came knocking, having a backbone meant more than just making tough decisions; it was about doing so with grit and a sprinkle of my own sass, respect, and a heavy dose of resilience. It's like being the anchor in a storm, standing firm in my convictions even when the waters got choppy. Leading with integrity became a guiding principle, a bit like having a moral compass that always pointed to my true north.

This backbone wasn't just a personal trait; it influenced the whole team. Picture it as a domino effect - when the leader stands strong, it inspires everyone else to find their backbone too. (Remember the rudderless CEO I wrote about prior? This is one antidote to being rudderless). It wasn't always easy, but facing uncertainties head-on and maintaining a sturdy leadership presence became the key way we tackled challenges.

Things were changing.

This example reflects the dynamic interplay of these elements in leadership – balancing the head (using your discernment), the heart (compassion) and backbone (grit).

By embracing the discomfort of new levels and new devils, I not only elevated my team but also developed my own leadership capabilities.

Are you leading with your head, your heart and your backbone?

I certainly was not initially. I was leading more with my heart and backbone and less with my head. I say that because I was mindful of always putting the people element as priority, and as the Head of People and Culture, I also had to balance the corporate needs in the mix. The head part was missing for me… That is the part that I especially had to develop.

I did so by focusing on the priorities of my team and balancing it with the upcoming workload. As I mentioned, the organisation I was at was growing rapidly. I had many conversations with my manager about our resourcing, priorities and the support that my team needed. I had the "if you want this work, what would you like to take off our to-do list" conversation. It freed up my team to focus on organisational growth and I managed to get two new people in my team for short-term projects.

Do you know what you have to develop? Your head? Your heart? Or your backbone?

How balanced is your leadership?

You may have completed a personality assessment or even had a 360 leadership assessment conducted. While those tools are great for self awareness, they don't expand to offer a more practical insight into the practical actions you could take. The upcoming activity is a practical one and may be a complementary addition to any personality or leadership assessment you may have conducted.

Activity: Head, Heart, and Backbone Self-Assessment

Reflect on the following questions to assess your leadership balance:

- How do I make decisions? (Head)
- How do I empathise with others? (Heart)
- How do I demonstrate courage? (Backbone)
- Where can I improve in balancing these aspects?

Introducing the Head, Heart, and Backbone Self-Assessment - a tool to explore essential aspects of your leadership style.

The "**Head**" invites contemplation on strategic thinking, decision-making, and goal alignment, encouraging a holistic perspective. Ever considered visualising your long-term goals or reflecting on decision outcomes?

Meanwhile, the "**Heart**" dimension delves into emotional intelligence, compassion, belonging and empathy, prompting reflection on active listening, team dynamics, and recognition practices. Curious about strategies for fostering genuine connections?

Lastly, the "**Backbone**" focuses on courage, resilience, and accountability. How comfortable are you with making brave decisions and navigating unexpected challenges?

This is a self-assessment tool for you to consider for yourself first and then re-do it for your team. I have provided you with practical suggestions to implement. You might have ideas of what to implement yourself; do whatever works. The key here is to conduct the self-assessment by answering the questions in the notes section provided and then to outline and determine the strategies that would suit you and the team you have in mind.

Head:

- ☐ **Strategic Thinking:** How often do you consider the long-term goals of your team or projects?
- ☐ **Decision-Making:** Reflect on recent decisions. Were they primarily based on analysis and strategy?
- ☐ **Knowledge Update:** How frequently do you invest time in updating your specialist skills to stay top of your game and your industry knowledge and skills?
- ☐ **Problem-Solving:** Consider recent challenges. Did you approach them with a strategic problem-solving mindset?
- ☐ **Big Picture Focus:** When faced with tasks, do you often connect them to the broader goals and vision?

Head - Practical Suggestions:

- ☐ **Strategy Board:** Create a visual board for long-term goals and ideas. Regularly update and revisit it. Call this "Your Own Strategic Plan."
- ☐ **Decision Journal:** Maintain a journal to track decisions, analyse outcomes, and learn from the process.
- ☐ **Learning Ritual:** Set aside time for reading, learn something new in your team meetings for 10 minutes as a repeat agenda item, listen to my Ways to Change the Workplace Podcast, do online courses, or attend industry events.
- ☐ **Goal Alignment:** Ensure that daily tasks align with the overarching goals of the team or organisation.

Heart:

- ☐ **Active Listening:** How often do you engage in active listening during team interactions?
- ☐ **Empathy Check:** Reflect on recent interactions and decisions that you have made. Did you consider the feelings and perspectives of others?
- ☐ **Recognition Practice:** How frequently do you express appreciation or recognise the efforts of your team?
- ☐ **Feedback Loop:** Evaluate your feedback style. Is it constructive, supportive, and focused on growth? Are you also asking your team for feedback on yourself?
- ☐ **Team Connection:** Reflect on team dynamics. Do you actively foster a sense of connection and camaraderie?

<u>Heart - Practical Suggestions:</u>

- ☐ **Listening Sessions:** Schedule regular one-on-one listening sessions with team members and key stakeholders and do something from the learnings.
- ☐ **Empathy Map:** Create an empathy map to understand the emotions and needs of team members and stakeholders. If you don't know what an empathy map is, there are plenty of free templates online; adapt one to suit you.
- ☐ **Kudos Board:** Establish a virtual or physical board to publicly acknowledge and celebrate achievements. We are too quick to move from one achievement to another without celebrating and learning.

- ☐ **Team Optimisation Sessions:** Work with a seasoned facilitator to hold a team optimisation session (as I call them) once a quarter. This enables your team to come up for air and to smell the roses, learn and pave the way forward with genuine engagement and it helps you and the team remain on the right track strategically. It just takes four days out of your work year. It is a no-brainer.

Backbone:

- ☐ **Decision Courage:** How comfortable are you with making tough decisions, even if they're unpopular?
- ☐ **Handling Criticism:** Reflect on your reaction to criticism. Are you open to constructive feedback?
- ☐ **Adaptability:** Consider recent challenges. Did you adapt your plans when faced with unexpected obstacles?
- ☐ **Ownership Mentality:** How often do you take responsibility for both successes and setbacks?
- ☐ **Staying Resilient:** Reflect on setbacks. How quickly do you bounce back and refocus on goals?

Backbone - Practical Suggestions:

- ☐ **Decision Dares:** Challenge yourself to make one decision outside your comfort zone each week – within the legal and ethical bounds of your workplace of course.
- ☐ **Feedback Journal:** Keep a journal to track feedback, analyse patterns, and set improvement goals; e.g. I used to keep a folder in my Outlook email and reflect on it once a month.

- ☐ **Adaptability Exercise:** List potential challenges and brainstorm alternative responses and react differently next time the same thing happens.
- ☐ **Ownership Mindset:** Foster a culture of accountability by openly acknowledging both successes and failures.
- ☐ **Resilience Rituals:** Develop personal resilience rituals, such as mindfulness exercises or gratitude journaling. You do whatever works for you.
- ☐ **Develop Your Team:** Work with a facilitator to hold a team optimisation session once a quarter as a non-negotiable. This is your team's chance to pause, reflect, and refocus. These sessions ensure everyone is engaged, aligned, and strategically on track. It's just four days a year—an essential investment for ongoing success.

Try the activity yourself and encourage individuals to regularly revisit and update their head, heart and backbone self-assessment, making it a dynamic tool to create meaningful workplaces. Choose three to five actionable strategies to focus on. Make sure they're realistic.

Chapter Recap

In this chapter, we've explored the importance of balanced leadership to create a culture that leaves a legacy. We also covered the concept of leading with head, heart, and backbone. By assessing your leadership balance and striving for improvement, you can ensure your decisions are well-rounded and effective.

Your Actions:

- ☐ Conduct the Head, Heart and Backbone Self-Assessment for yourself as an individual and determine the way forward from what you have noted.
- ☐ Conduct the Head, Heart and Backbone Self-Assessment for your team and determine the way forward from what you have noted.
- ☐ Choose three to five strategies to work on; ensure you choose something achievable.
- ☐ Prepare for the next chapter, where we'll explore culture optimisation beyond surveys.

Notes:

PART 3 of Make Work Meaningful: Sustaining Your Legacy

CHAPTER 9

Culture Optimisation Beyond Surveys

> **Chapter Overview**
>
> Many people overuse and rely solely on culture or engagement tools which leads to a culture that is not effectively yours. In this chapter, I cover a case study of one of the best CEOs I have had the pleasure to support on his ongoing journey of culture optimisation. I share the concept of a psychological contract and how you can tap into it by creating moments that matter.

Beyond Surveys

Surveys and tools can provide valuable insights, but they are not enough to create a meaningful legacy. Understanding and addressing psychological contracts— the unwritten expectations between employers and employees— is crucial for sustaining a positive culture.

The number of organisations that use culture survey tools, or psychometric tools as their security blanket is shocking to me. It is like a cook with only one recipe. Limited and reliant upon the same old boring ingredients. This recipe lacks flair, originality and your own flavour.

Many organisations have impersonal language to describe their culture. The language which is used comes from an overreliance on said culture or engagement survey tools. There is a missing piece in personalising the way you optimise your culture and that is what I will cover in this chapter.

As opposed to an employee mission and values all written in your vernacular. Then comes culture survey time and the language used is that of an external culture survey provider. The missing piece is working with what you've already got.

Most organisations spend thousands on culture tools, consultants, and fleeting trends to pacify survey respondents who may have expressed discontent. The truth is, your people detect the insincerity if nothing is done when your results are announced; it reeks.

People's radars are on and their psychological contract with your workplace is on thin ice. Consider yourself placed on notice by your people.

Psychological Contracts, They Will Make or Break Your Culture

The concept of the psychological contract was originally developed by Denise Rousseau, the H. J. Heinz II University Professor of Organisational Behaviour and Public Policy at Carnegie Mellon University.

Unlike a formal employee contract, a psychological contract is a covert, implied, unwritten set of hopes that the employee has. Each one of us will have a different psychological contract with our workplace. It includes values, mutual beliefs, common ground and expectations between the employer and employee. It is unwritten and often in the mind of the employee. And it is always evolving (as we evolve).

The link between psychological contracts and your organisational culture is immense.

It is the glue that binds the employee to your purpose, vision, mission, values and to all the good stuff.

An employee with a positive psychological contract will be:

- More agile (as your organisation changes, so will the employee).
- More loyal (they won't be job hunting).
- More productive (they know what they have to do and how they fit into the bigger picture).
- More customer focused (they know the bottom line).

As opposed to an employee with a negative psychological contract, who will more likely be:

- Disengaged or unproductive
- Negative or toxic
- Looking for work elsewhere
- Less open to change
- Negatively impacting your bottom line

That's why you must cultivate your culture beyond the confines of surveys and psychometrics; to create an enduring, genuine team spirit and organisational culture that withstands the test of time, far beyond any tool.

Case Study: Anthony Vuleta's Way

Anthony Vuleta, a CEO I worked with, understood the importance of psychological contracts. By listening to his people and focusing on creating moments that matter, he has been able to foster a positive and lasting organisational culture.

Given individuals have a psychological contract with work, how will you enable your workplace culture to tap into their true needs? The answer is to move beyond sole reliance on a culture survey tool.

By this stage you may have articulated your desired culture. If not, all good, but do work on that after you have finished reading.

The Town of Victoria Park is a town just outside of the central business district of Perth. It has a very distinct feel and vibe to it in terms of arts and culture and the food scene. The people of the Town of Victoria Park Council rightly take great pride in the town that they serve.

I have had the pleasure of supporting CEO, Anthony Vuleta, and various teams of The Town of Victoria Park Council for several years and I noticed something different about them from the get go.

I remember my first meeting with Anthony. He was all about organisational culture, so much so that he proudly showed me his organisation's past culture champion trophies prized to them from culture survey providers. They had significant shifts and a positive culture. He was rightly very proud of his people and clearly believed in leading and continually building and investing in his organisation's culture. When I met him, he had even created a role in his People and Culture team: an Organisational Development Consultant to focus on said culture. Whoa. What a dream, I thought.

What I came to learn by observing Anthony, by working with him, by having him as my guest on my Ways to Change the Workplace Podcast (episodes 29 and 99) is that Anthony is focused on leaving a legacy for the sector in which he works. His vision goes beyond the immediate, beyond what lies in front of him; he intends to leave a lasting legacy for the local government sector that he serves. He has expanded his circle beyond his organisation. Anthony thinks big and you can see it in the small things that he does too.

He is a CEO who has taken on nurturing his culture to transcend the limitations of culture survey tools, and I have seen it foster a lasting and heartfelt organisational and team spirit.

Anthony is widely praised throughout the organisation:

- An employee from the town's library team told me they appreciated how Anthony personally called to check on them and their families during a horrific bushfire scare.
- Those who have left the company feel that Anthony genuinely considered and acted upon the feedback they provided him upon their departure.
- Leaders acknowledge Anthony's encouragement to apply for challenging secondments in other areas.

Caveat: Anthony doesn't always get it right, and he admits it. He likes to try new things, to continually optimise his culture, to experiment, so failure is an expected part of this, and he is okay with failure as long as he and his people learn from it.

I have noticed that Anthony is focused on two things: listening, and developing others to benefit the sector that he serves.

That is Anthony's way as I have observed and experienced it. What is your way?

By listening, he understands, and can then make the right decisions, plans or next steps.

As an illustration, he has continued the practice of hosting online all-staff town hall meetings for two key reasons:

1. The sessions are recorded, offering flexibility for participants to watch later or to join remotely.
2. Another significant advantage of these online meetings is the straightforward and clever analysis of the data collected during the session, which I'll now elaborate on.

What Anthony does at the end of the meeting is ask a big question to get the sentiment of the employees. Questions, such as, "what do you feel you need to develop on?" or, "what could we as a leadership team do differently?" or even a question as straightforward as, "how are you doing today?"

Anthony then asks his people and culture team to collate the responses and put them into a word cloud which gives him a quick visual on the common themes. What I do know from these forums, is the staff have been developed on things they asked for, some leadership ways have changed, and it is a constant work in progress. Not all wishes are always granted at work, but what can be dealt with is acted upon there and then – not when the next culture survey runs.

This is not a set and forget type of managing organisational culture; culture is always on Anthony's radar.

Thanks to this approach, Anthony always has a current baseline picture of what his people's general sentiments are. He is also approachable, and he has an open-door policy at certain times for anyone to pop in to see him for a chat. Anthony and his team work beyond culture survey tools, *they have created their own way.*

Not everyone is like Anthony or his people.

But you can easily start now, whether you are a CEO, a leader or a team member... You can make moments that matter.

Making Moments That Matter

How can you nurture your culture to transcend the limitations of culture survey tools?

Firstly, listen to what your people are saying. Create a genuine dialogue. Then with that data, do something about it. Create moments that matter.

I have broken down the upcoming sections for relevance for CEOs, leaders or for teams. I recommend you read each section and consider what solutions best apply for you. As always, choose what suits your culture or get creative to see what other ideas you get.

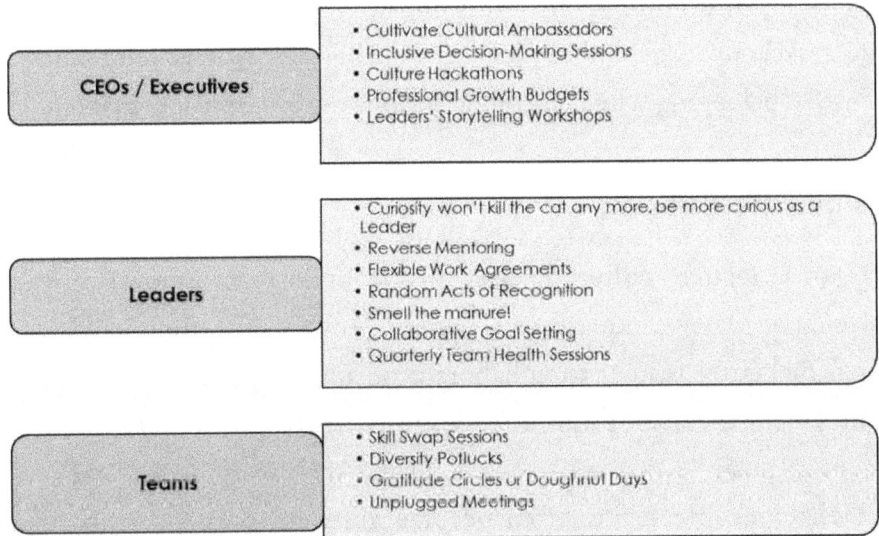

For CEOs:

Cultivate Cultural Ambassadors:

Identify individuals across different levels who embody the desired culture. Empower them as cultural ambassadors to influence their peers positively. Encourage them to share stories and initiatives that align with the company's values and decide how else you would like to utilise these people.

Inclusive Decision-Making Sessions:

Foster a culture of inclusivity by including diverse voices in key decisions. Create a platform for open discussions where employees can contribute ideas. Acknowledge and implement valuable suggestions, reinforcing a sense of belonging which encourages collaborative decision-making.

Culture Hackathons:

Organise regular "culture hackathons" to brainstorm innovative ways to enhance the workplace environment. Invite cross-functional (and even bickering teams) to collaborate on quick, impactful initiatives. Implement the most promising ideas swiftly to demonstrate commitment to positive change. I have delivered such sessions, and they are FUN. Opposing teams often become allies for each other, barriers break down, and so do silos.

Professional Growth Budgets:

Allocate budgets for employees' professional development. Encourage them to invest in learning experiences that align with both their aspirations and the company's values. This investment not only benefits individuals but also contributes to a culture of continuous learning. In tough financial or societal times, the learning budget is the first to be chopped. That is a dumb decision because during these times is exactly when you should be developing; you ought to be developing your people to enable cutting-edge thinking.

Leaders' Storytelling Workshops:

Conduct workshops on the art of storytelling. Encourage leaders to share personal stories that connect with the company's culture (or desired culture, hello). This fosters a sense of authenticity and builds a narrative that employees can relate to on a genuine level. This also creates your own organisation's collective rhetoric, going beyond the rhetoric provided to you from the culture survey or psychometric tools.

For Leaders:

Curiosity won't kill the cat anymore, be more curious as a Leader:

Prioritise a new style of leadership by actively and GENUINELY seeking to understand team members' perspectives. Listen. Have regular one-on-one check-ins. This is about fostering a supportive culture. Start to change the way you listen and the way you connect, understand, work, relate, and get on with others will also change… This requires you to de-clench and let go of whatever your narrative is about being a leader and start from a blank sheet. This skill is simple to comprehend, yet often very hard for many leaders to grapple with. But if you nail this part, you're in for a wild fun ride.

Reverse Mentoring:

Implement reverse mentoring programs where junior employees mentor leaders on emerging trends and diverse perspectives. This dynamic exchange promotes a culture of mutual respect and continuous learning.

Flexible Work Agreements:

Offer flexible work arrangements that prioritise outcomes over hours. Can we please move beyond the traditional bum on seat clock-watching conversation? Trust employees to manage their time effectively, promoting a culture of accountability and work-life integration. We are all more than our jobs.

Random Acts of Recognition:

Encourage other leaders to acknowledge and celebrate your team's small wins and efforts regularly. Reach out and ask for feedback. Random acts of recognition, such as personalised thank-you notes, emails, or a simple verbal thanks all build a positive and appreciative culture. We are all too quick to move from one milestone to another without taking a pause to smell the roses (and the manure). Roses are what I am talking about here.

Smell the Manure!

It happens. Stuff will go wrong. Learn from it by holding post-mortem sessions for understanding issues, or ideally to build into your leadership toolkit. Address said issues. By building a culture of reflection, behaviour or process change as a result and learning from our mistakes, we start to leave a good trail for our legacy.

Collaborative Goal Setting:

I used to hate the scripted goal setting sessions with one of my managers because they didn't listen. They verbally vomited their expectations onto my performance plan with no input or say from me. It was a waste of my life. I get it, this manager hated the process and wanted to be as quick as possible to tick the box. Still not cool. If you too are like my ex-manager, and loathe the goal setting process, do it with respect, it will be less painful for all. Involve team members in the goal-setting process to ensure alignment with individual and team aspirations. Foster a collaborative approach that encourages shared ownership and commitment to achieving common objectives. Having a clear line of sight as to how one fits into the bigger picture goes a long way in developing a positive organisational culture beyond reliance on culture survey tools.

Quarterly Team Optimisation Sessions:

Choose a skilled and trusted facilitator to enable you and your team to come up for air, to be strategic, to bond, to have fun and to have the right kinds of conversations – the conversations that you *need* to have. I have partnered with teams as their facilitator for years in this manner and I have delivered all sorts of sessions. I tailor the session to suit the team I am supporting, and they have ranged from: getting to know each other through psychometric tests, strategic creative planning through to sessions and conversations on emotional contagion. You name it. These sessions should allow you to take a forward-thinking approach and enliven you all as a team. It also enables you to have the collective conversations that you need to. Having such sessions quarterly only takes up four days a year. It's a no-brainer but many teams still do not gather in this manner. It is important for the leader to be there as a participant and use a trusted facilitator to run these sessions. Take your leader hat off; it is refreshing.

For Team Members:

Skill Swap Sessions:

Initiate skill swap sessions where team members teach each other skills. This not only promotes a culture of continuous learning but also builds stronger interpersonal connections.

Diversity Potlucks:

Organise cultural potluck events where team members bring dishes representing their cultural backgrounds. This fosters an inclusive environment and celebrates diversity in a tangible way. I used to do this in a job when I first moved to Perth in Western Australia in 2008 and I still drool at the memory of Marks' wife's Thai curries. We have a common connection and people bond over food. Breaking bread was a thing long before my and your time. Eating together is a norm in many cultures and there is something about this act that enables us to connect with each other at a deeper level.

Gratitude Circles or Doughnut Days:

Form small "gratitude circles" where team members regularly express appreciation for each other's contributions. Cultivating a culture of gratitude enhances teamwork and positive collaboration. You work out what works for you. For some teams a thank you jar full of post it notes read out at team meetings may be too cringey; try other things, such as doughnut days. I did exactly this to celebrate our achievements (yes, even when it was the two of us in my team, me and the wonderful Chris back in the day, doughnut days were a thing). You choose what will suit the culture, taste and cringe needs of your team.

Unplugged Meetings:

Designate specific meetings as "unplugged" sessions where digital devices are put aside. This encourages focused, meaningful conversations and helps build deeper connections among team members. I enable this when I facilitate sessions. Bonus tip: Instead of typing on a device to take notes, try a white board or flipchart! The power of writing opens your mind, ears and eyes like you would not believe.

People often complain to me that they have no decision-making power or say over the way the organisational culture is. I hope I have just shown you how you do have control and *can* nurture your culture or create a subculture at whatever level you are without reliance on any culture survey tools.

Whether you are a CEO, leader or team member you certainly can nurture your culture to transcend the limitations of culture survey tools, fostering a lasting and heartfelt organisational or team spirit. Go forth and prosper with the legacy that you wish to leave to make work meaningful.

Activity: Reflective Questions on Optimising Culture

Use these questions to reflect on your approach to culture optimisation:

- How do I address psychological contracts in my organisation?
- What moments matter most to my people?
- How can I create and sustain a positive culture?

- What actions can I take to go beyond reliance on traditional surveys and tools?

> **Chapter Recap**
>
> In this chapter, we've explored the importance of optimising culture beyond surveys and tools. By understanding and addressing psychological contracts, you can create a positive and lasting organisational culture. The story of CEO Anthony Vuleta gave you an insight into practical ways you can create your own narrative around culture – beyond reliance on culture surveys and such tools. By having your own rhetoric on how you intend to make work meaningful in this context (or by creating your own way) you can build a culture that resonates with everyone.
>
> **Your Actions:**
>
> ☐ You are more than a culture survey tool – determine which "Moments That Matter" options you will choose (and how you will implement them) and don't take your foot off the pedal.
>   ☐ Ensure you put at least two ideas in place.
> ☐ Implement strategies to address psychological contracts.
> ☐ Determine how you will keep your organisational culture always on your radar.
> ☐ Prepare for the next chapter, where we'll discuss managing plot twists.

Notes:

CHAPTER 10

Managing Plot Twists

> **Chapter Overview**
>
> Creating a meaningful culture is not a smooth journey. This chapter explores the types of career plot twists you may encounter. We will explore practical strategies for managing the unexpected in your professional journey. From cultivating adaptability to fostering a mindset of continuous learning, you'll discover ways to transform plot twists into pivotal moments for growth and advancement.

Navigating the Unexpected

Career plot twists are inevitable. Whether it's an unexpected job change, a challenging project, or a personal setback, how you navigate these twists can impact your legacy.

Rudyard Kipling in his poem titled If wrote a profound line which slapped me around the face like you would not believe when I first read it. I am a planner. I like to visualise, strategise and actualise to make things happen.

Rudyard Kipling's powerful line from his poem If, "If you can dream and not make dreams your master," resonates with those who thrive on planning and execution without being attached to their grand plans. How can your dreams NOT be your master, I asked? Once you understand it, it makes total sense. It's a profound reminder that while dreams and aspirations are essential, they shouldn't become dictators of our actions and choices.

It is a lesson in going with the flow, and with the plot twists.

If you're a person who enjoys visualising, strategising, and actualising plans, you understand the value of turning dreams into reality.

Kipling's line, "If you can dream and not make dreams your master," serves as a cautionary note against letting the allure of dreams control and overshadow the reality of what is happening in front of you.

Dreams are the spores of ambition, the sparks that ignite our passions and propel us forward. But plot twists will happen, you cannot avoid or ignore them. That's life.

Your ability to plan and execute is undoubtedly an asset, but it is crucial to maintain a delicate balance.

It's about acknowledging the power of dreams while recognising that they should serve as guides rather than rulers. (Read this line again).

In the attempt to turn aspirations into accomplishments, there's a dance between imagination and action. It's about holding onto the vision while being grounded in the realities and practicalities of planning and execution as well as the reality of what is happening around us right now. Kipling's wisdom encourages embracing dreams as *partners* in your journey, not as *masters* that dictate every step.

It won't be smooth sailing all the way.

Life, including our work life, much like all good stories, is riddled with unexpected plot twists. In your career and professional journey, there will undoubtedly be moments when the plot takes a twist, or in the past has taken an unforeseen turn.

Life happens. People change. Things change. Road bumps and detours are expected.

How can you develop the ability to navigate and manage difficult circumstances when events deviate from the expected script?

As Shakespeare astutely noted, "The course of true love never did run smooth." While originally applied to matters of the heart, this sentiment is equally applicable to the twists and turns encountered in the world of work. Just as love demands resilience and adaptability, so too does the path to our professional fulfilment if we wish to remain on course to making work meaningful.

Let's expand this line of thinking with a quote from Steve Jobs:

"Your work is going to fill a large part of your life, and the only way to be truly satisfied is to do what you believe is great work."

In the grand narrative of your career, challenges and unexpected events are the plot twists that add depth and complexity and a touch of spice to your career. I have had plenty so far and plenty more are going to come my way. Just as true love requires effort and commitment, so does achieving satisfaction in your professional life.

The truth is, it is not hunky dory all the time. You're not constantly smelling the roses. Sometimes there'll be a nasty smell around.

The ability to manage plot twists is a skill that distinguishes those who merely endure their careers from those who truly thrive in the face of adversity and remain focused on the legacy that they wish to leave.

When confronted with an unexpected twist in your career journey, consider it a plot development or plot twist, rather than a roadblock.

Case Study: Common Career Plot Twists

Let's explore some common career plot twists and questions for you to consider navigating them. These examples will provide insights into unexpected changes and consideration for you to maintain your momentum.

Plot Twist - New Industry Trends:

- A sudden shift in industry trends or market demands forces you to reassess your career trajectory, or the way you are working. The rate of change is exponential and impacting workplaces dramatically. In today's fast-paced world, industries evolve swiftly, requiring individuals to adapt to emerging trends or face professional stagnation. Do you remember Kodak? What happened to them was a result of not keeping up with industry trends in the world of photography. Smart phones, the rise of social media and digital cameras won this race over Kodak's now redundant cameras.

Plot Twist - Being Dragged Along:

- Unexpected promotions or leadership opportunities that come with new responsibilities and challenges. Perhaps you will be dragged into your next role due to your brilliance (and not drive it yourself, we covered this earlier). Many individuals find themselves unexpectedly thrust into leadership or new project roles, necessitating a rapid adjustment to leading new challenges, new teams and making crucial decisions. Have you been thrown into the deep end without a life jacket?

Plot Twist - Skill Set Shake-Up:

- Rapid technological advancements or industry changes demand us to acquire new skills or update existing ones. Staying relevant in a dynamic job market often requires adapting to new technologies or acquiring additional expertise. Just think of how we have moved from fax to email to instant messaging (and it continues beyond that). The way we work and communicate has therefore also evolved and those not keeping up with these changes are falling behind.

Plot Twist - Team Turbulence:

- Sudden changes in team dynamics, such as restructuring, disagreements or leadership changes can lead to unforeseen challenges. Team dynamics can significantly impact work satisfaction; navigating these changes requires interpersonal skills and adaptability. Think back through your career, how many times did the executive have a great idea, or even a brain fart of an idea, which changed the direction of your team or project? Or how many times have you come across, or worked in a dysfunctional team?

Plot Twist - The Unexpected Detour:

- Life happens. Personal or external factors, like health or family issues or economic downturns, create unexpected disruptions in career plans. Life's uncertainties can affect professional paths, requiring resilience and a strategic approach to overcome unexpected obstacles. A great example here is that of the Baby Boomer generation. Many are still holding onto their jobs due to the past economic downturns. Workforce planners did not expect Baby Boomers to hold on to their jobs for as long as they have. This has certainly been an unexpected plot twist.

Activity: The Revolutionary Act of Weekly Self-Coaching to Keep Your Legacy Goal in Check

Remember the page that you dog-eared, or bookmarked earlier on? Refer to that as you conduct this activity as part of your weekly routine.

This has been a game changer for me. I tried it for months myself, then I tested it on my coaching clients and since then I have self-published a Self-Coaching Journal titled: You Can't Stop a Shooting Star.

YOU are the shooting star.

Self-coaching is taking time out of your day, ideally once a week, to reflect on your learnings, your achievements, your goals and to plan how you are going to achieve those goals.

This is a conscious reflection to pause and observe how you have behaved, what you have learned and what your wins were.

This activity will also allow you to focus on your challenges, actions for accountability and planning.

All of my coachees have found this one of the most useful tools to apply at the end of their week. This is a great example of how one can self-coach with huge impact.

Not only will it develop your emotional intelligence and all of the soft skills which are really hard; you will also develop your relationships and your perspectives. It will allow you to stay on course amidst the calm and definitely amidst the storms that you may face.

I do this once a week, on a Friday afternoon as I am planning the approaching week. I recommend you try it on a Friday afternoon for 30 minutes. I know you will get a lot from it once you start to practise it weekly.

For me, it has become a part of my weekly habits and I could not do without it.

Tip: Schedule 30 minutes in your calendar, ideally at the end of each week to do this. Once you establish self-coaching as a habit, you're going to be sharing it with your team, your peers and the world!

I write the responses to these questions in my Self-Coaching Journal; you decide what works for you.

The act of writing and looking back at my progress has been fundamental in helping me to better appreciate my achievements, to manage plot twists and to push forward with the legacy goal that I have determined.

Self-Coaching Questions to Ask Yourself Each Week:

1. **What am I learning?**
   Tip: Emotionally intelligent people view everything as a learning opportunity, even the sh1t stuff.

2. **How am I, today, right now? How has my week been?**
   Note: This is how I start off my coaching sessions to see where my coachees are at. Do you check in on where you are at?

3. **What were my wins? What has felt like success?**
   Note: I believe in starting with the positives!

4. **What are my triggers, challenges and what can I do to mitigate them? What may have taken me off the course of creating my legacy?**
   Note: This is what I support my coachees through. I ask the tough questions they may be avoiding or may not have

considered. They then agree on actions to take which they will be accountable for.

5. **What do I want to be held accountable for next week?**
   Fun fact: This is what I check in on the next time we have a coaching appointment. Think of a coach as your guide to progress in your professional career. My coachees always have so much to report back. Be your own coach!

6. **What needs planning? What important things have no action steps attached to them?**
   Tip: Here are some of the questions I ask my coachees to ensure they are on the path to success and have the support and resources that they need:

   - Do you need help? Who do you need to engage with to make this happen?
   - What is stopping you?
   - How are you going to celebrate when you have achieved what you need to?

So, continue to dream big, visualise your goals, and craft meticulous plans. Just remember that your dreams should inspire and guide you, not become chains that restrict your adaptability and resilience in the face of unexpected plot twists and turns.

As you navigate the path from vision to reality, let your dreams fuel your determination to leave your legacy without losing sight of the pragmatic steps needed to bring it to life. By referring back to your dog-eared or bookmarked page with your defined legacy goal, you can keep sight of how you intend to make work more meaningful.

Use this activity to stay focused on your legacy goals, even during challenging times.

> **Chapter Recap**
>
> In this chapter, we've discussed the inevitability of career plot twists and strategies for navigating them. Things happen, life happens, but you can still stay on course. By staying focused on your legacy goal and using self-coaching techniques, you can maintain momentum and continue to make meaningful progress.
>
> **Your Actions:**
>
> - ☐ Complete the Weekly Self-Coaching Activity. Build this into your weekly schedule for 30 minutes each week. I do it on a Friday morning and I link it to my to-do list for the upcoming week. Try it and let me know how you go!
> - ☐ Implement strategies to navigate career plot twists.
> - ☐ Prepare for the next chapter, where we'll explore knowing when to leave and pass the baton.

Notes:

CHAPTER 11

Knowing When to Leave and Pass the Baton

> **Chapter Overview**
>
> All good things come to an end. This chapter explores the importance of recognising when it's time to leave and how to pass the baton effectively. By the end of this chapter, you'll have practical strategies for ensuring a smooth transition and leaving a lasting legacy.

Recognising When to Leave

Knowing when to leave a role or organisation is crucial for maintaining a positive legacy. It's important to recognise the signs and make a strategic decision to move on at the right time.

How long do you intend on being in this job?

That is the question I used to ask myself in all of my corporate jobs. It is an important question to ask as we all have an expiry date workwise too.

Have you heard about the CEO who clung to their job for years as if it were their lifeline, the very essence of their identity? They couldn't fathom leaving, fearing it would brand them as failures.

The thing is, you have to let go and pass the baton eventually.

I have supported many CEOs who have been in their roles for years. The longest serving one was nearing 20 years at one company and there was a lot of learning from that CEO.

While they gave their people and their stakeholders certainty and a sense of confidence in the future, things also went a bit stale.

People depended on the CEO a lot more than they should have.

People stopped giving ideas due to lack of motivation and oomph.

Have you heard the story of The Emperor's New Clothes?

The Emperor's New Clothes is a classic fairy tale by Hans Christian Andersen. The story revolves around an emperor who is overly concerned with his appearance. Two weavers trick him into believing they have made him a suit of clothes that is invisible to those who are unfit for their positions, stupid, or incompetent.

In reality, there is no suit, but the Emperor, afraid to admit he can't see it, parades through the town in his imaginary attire (in the nude, yep, butt naked). It takes an innocent child to point out the truth (I imagine Nelson from The Simpson's voice saying, "ha ha" and pointing at the butt naked Emperor).

With the Emperor's lack of clothing exposed, the townspeople realise they were holding back on speaking the truth due to fear of hierarchy and the positional power that the Emperor had. The tale is often interpreted as a commentary on vanity, arrogance, and the fear of speaking out against authority.

With the CEO being there for two decades, it created an unhealthy co-dependency which reflected externally too. Everyone knew what to expect and if things went awry, the people would rely on the CEO to sort it. They wouldn't speak out or offer new ideas, or even challenge the status quo. Everyone in the organisation was on cruise control.

What the CEO stopped doing was being interested, being intrigued and being fresh with ideas. They went stale and it affected their professional brand.

They stopped learning and connecting with their higher purpose of leaving a legacy due to the fact that they were comfortable with their life, their salary and the perceived status they had. I worked with the CEO to give them the kick start they needed to end their career on a positive with their internal people and external stakeholders. They left the organisation with their head held high and the farewell and kudos that they deserved.

I worked with the CEO to ensure that they left the organisation better than they started with. I did an audit of what the CEO wanted to achieve personally for themselves (the 'Me' factor), for their executive team (the 'We' factor), and for the organisation and industry at large (the 'Us' factor). I'll cover what Me, We and Us refer to in more detail later in this chapter.

I learned that the CEO was yet to achieve the individual goal of empowering aspiring leaders for the success of the future of the organisation. These were not the CEO's successors but the successors of the successors. These were people who had potential, these were the legacy believers and the legacy dreamers that I wrote about earlier. The CEO wanted a talent pipeline which was adequately prepared for the evolution of the organisation and the industry. I worked with the CEO to understand the needs of this group of aspiring leaders and the essential missing piece for them was upskilling on soft skills, which, let's be honest, are the hardest skills to often learn. Skills such as self-awareness, emotional intelligence and the ability to connect and communicate with people at all levels. We created the Aspiring Leaders Program which was such a success that I rolled out two rounds of the program. It created lasting connections and camaraderie between peers and started to organically break silos.

The CEO also had a desire to address unsaid issues in their executive team and we worked together through executive team coaching to iron out said crinkles. There are many things that executive teams need to address but rarely do, such as establishing trust, nurturing open communication, aligning on strategic priorities, and fostering a culture of accountability. We conducted insightful sessions that encouraged frank discussions and constructive feedback. Our aim was to create a safe environment where vulnerabilities could be acknowledged and transformed into opportunities for growth.

A pivotal moment in our coaching journey occurred when the CEO recognised the importance of vulnerability in leadership. They shared personal anecdotes of challenges faced and lessons learned, setting a powerful example for their team. This change in leadership style had a ripple effect, inspiring greater transparency, and empathy within the executive.

Another critical area we addressed was decision-making dynamics within the team. We explored methods to streamline processes, clarified roles, and empowered individuals to make informed decisions aligned with the organisation's vision. By promoting a culture of collective ownership, the executive team became more agile and responsive to market changes.

Through our collaborative efforts, the executive team evolved into a cohesive unit, driven by shared values and a collective vision. They emerged stronger, more resilient, and better equipped to navigate the complexities of leadership in a rapidly evolving landscape as the CEO departed.

The CEO wanted to give back to the industry in which they worked and therefore decided to volunteer to be a mentor for those in the industry. Through this initiative, the CEO not only contributed to the development of individuals, but also strengthened the fabric of the industry as a whole. Their dedication to mentoring exemplified a genuine commitment to paying it forward and creating a positive ripple effect that extended far beyond their tenure.

This act of giving back underscored the CEO's ethos of leaving a lasting impact - a legacy that transcended organisational boundaries and enriched the lives and careers of countless individuals within the industry.

This partnership excelled traditional coaching boundaries. It was characterised by introspection, empowerment, and meaningful connections. Together, we redefined success not just in terms of tenure but in the enduring impact we leave on those we inspire and empower. This CEO was intent on making work meaningful again for the organisation.

The CEO's departure marked not an end but a new beginning – an opportunity for the organisation to embrace change, cultivate talent, and continue the legacy of visionary leadership. And for me, it was a testament to the profound impact we can achieve when we dare to challenge norms and invest in the growth of ourselves as individuals, organisations and our industries.

Whether you are a CEO, a leader or in a team, ideally this is your mission – to leave the organisation better off, never worse off and to not overstay.

So how does one go about that?

Have you ever considered it for yourself?

In the quest to leave an organisation better than you found it, one must first acknowledge the power of positive influence. As a CEO, leader, or team member, embracing a mindset that values growth, sustainability, and positive impact becomes paramount.

Consider this: your leadership journey is not just about achieving personal success but fostering an environment where everyone can thrive. It's about cultivating a culture of collaboration, innovation, and continuous improvement. Whether you're steering the ship as a CEO or contributing as a team member, the collective goal should be to enhance the organisation's DNA.

And when you are done, it is time to move on. Move on to retirement, move on to another job, move on to be your own boss – whatever it is, *it is imperative to know when you need to leave.*

Activity: Knowing When to Leave Questions

This is a personal example from myself. Each time I worked out when to leave a position, I utilised this methodology using the Me, We and Us concepts which I will now outline.

I break the below questions into:

Me – the needs for me as an individual.

We – the needs for us as a team.

Us – the needs for us as an organisation.

Have I met the needs for Me?

- Did I get the development I needed?
- Am I a different person?
- Have I learnt from my highs and lows?

- How have I effectively contributed to the legacy goal that I / we as a team wished to leave?

Have I met the needs for We, the team?

- Have I set up a solid team structure (or processes if you are an individual)?
- How have I contributed positively to my team's efforts?
- Have I focused beyond myself?
- Who have I been an ally for and opened doors for?
- Who is my successor and how am I upskilling or briefing them?

Have I met the needs for Us, the organisation, industry, or beyond?

- Have I (or if reading as a team, we) left a voice that resonates which goes beyond the usual corporate jargon?
- Have we defined our desired culture and made strides to achieve it / or are on the way to achieving it?
- Am I leaving the team / organisation better than when I started?
- Am I happy with the legacy that I am leaving?

Case Study: Effective Knowledge Transfer

Bonus tips once you have worked out when to leave:

You have now worked out that it is time to hand in your resignation. Congratulations, you legend.

If at all possible, plan ahead and give advance notice. This is in order to line everything up for your departure.

Have you heard of the concept of being "demob happy?"

Being demob happy is originally a military term and is defined either as:

1. feeling elated in anticipation of demobilization from the armed forces,

OR

2. feeling elated and carefree in anticipation of the end of any onerous or unpleasant period.

I am going to add a third definition to this with my poetic licence.

3. Demob happy is a feeling of freedom and excitement for all that you have achieved and wish to pass on.

I added the above definition myself as each time I resigned from a job with ample notice, things shifted: I knew I could step back from the delivery of work and work on my legacy to pass the baton. I had a clear end goal in mind and I continued to do great work to leave great plans I had. Consider whether you can give advance notice, longer than contractually deemed necessary. Why? So you can take your foot off the pedal and start to upskill and uplift your successor and the teams who you will be passing your work on to. This period is one of the best I have ever experienced when I was in corporate jobs – there's nothing like passing on the baton *properly*. I know that not everyone will have the luxury of a longer resignation period. If that is the case, the rest still applies.

That leads me to how does one pass the baton *properly*?

No doubt your organisation has exit procedures and processes. Blah blah and yawn is what I say to most of those exit procedures because they are lacklustre and lack basic human needs in most cases. They are often a tick in the human resources compliance box activity.

To combat that, I have helped many an organisation to think differently. By the time people leave the workplace, what they have achieved is far more than what was on their job description. The tacit knowledge they have is of immense value to the workplace.

Tacit knowledge is all of the unspoken, implicit and inferred stuff you do in your job – it is your way of doing things that has worked and served you and your workplace well. It is all of the stuff that is in your head, rather than documented, or in your job description. Think about it in *your* job. I bet you do far more than the words on your job description.

This is what often gets missed out in the traditional exit processes at work and it is detrimental to the success of the next person filling your shoes. So how to combat that?

Bonus Activity: Knowledge Transfer Plan

Create a knowledge transfer plan to ensure a smooth transition:

- Identify key knowledge areas and skills to transfer.
- Develop a timeline and process for transferring knowledge.
- Identify and train successors.
- Document important information and processes.

Identifying Critical Tasks and Activities

There are probably some aspects of your work that only you know how to do; that is the tacit knowledge that you are taking with you. It is essential to develop a list of those tasks and activities.

Below are some questions for your consideration before you answer the questions in the box below:

What are you known for?

If you left your position today, what wouldn't get done because no one else knows how to do it or what to do?

When you return from annual leave, what work is usually waiting for you because no one else knows how to do it?

When you are away from work, what do you worry about (what work isn't getting done or what work isn't being done well)?

What does your team rely on you for? What are you the "go-to" person for?

List the tasks and activities below using as many rows as necessary	List the critical knowledge, experience, or skill needed for this task	Is this a critical task? Y/N

Developing A Knowledge Transfer Plan

You don't want anyone to drop the ball after you leave, so therefore, for the tasks identified as **critical** on the table above, work with the right person (your boss, human resources or your successor) to develop a strategy for addressing that area.

Critical Tasks From Step 1 Above	Importance Low-Medium-High Gauge the importance of the task identified	Availability Is this knowledge and expertise currently available from anyone else in our work area? Yes, No, or Don't Know [if yes, who?]	Impact Low Medium High [If the task is important and there is no one else who possesses the knowledge, impact is high.]	Resources What resources [files, people, websites, references, resources, etc.] exist to help others learn this task? Add a link to where the files are saved.	Strategy How do you plan to address this knowledge gap? Who will learn it? How and when?
Example: Actioning our desired culture upskilling sessions.	*Example:* High	*Example:* No. Jane knows how to book the sessions, but I do the rest of the facilitation and data analysis.	*Example:* High	*Example:* Jane for booking. My handover notes and workshop plans are outlined in the shared drive.	*Example:* Outline step-by-step process of the workshops. Mentor and develop Lindsay to ensure he knows the process and can deliver the

						sessions. Jane is our key admin contact for this project. Creating a matrix of each person's expertise to help with the next stage of our desired culture strategy sessions by end of the week.

Leave with your head held high knowing that you have left a legacy.

It is not over yet, there is a final chapter to show you the way of legends.

Chapter Recap

In this chapter, we've explored the importance of recognising when to leave and how to pass the baton effectively. By creating a knowledge transfer plan, you can ensure a smooth transition and leave a lasting positive impact.

Your Actions:

- ☐ Before you resign, conduct the activity titled "Knowing When to Leave Questions."
- ☐ Hand in your resignation – with extra notice where possible.
- ☐ Upskill your successor if they are in place.
- ☐ Complete the knowledge transfer activity.
- ☐ Take your foot off the pedal and see all you have accomplished in leaving your legacy in this workplace.
- ☐ If you are moving onto another job, start this book again and strap yourself in.
- ☐ Prepare for the final chapter, where we'll explore how the show will go on.

Notes:

CHAPTER 12

The Show Will Go On

> **Chapter Overview**
>
> This final chapter focuses on the continuation of your legacy. We'll explore strategies for ensuring that your impact endures long after you've moved on. By the end of this chapter, you'll have a clear understanding of how to make work meaningful.

The Continuation of Legacy

Creating a meaningful legacy is about more than just the time you spend in a role. It's about the lasting impact you leave and how your contributions continue to influence others.

Now consider how far you have come. Well done on all your hard work and on putting the learnings from this book into place.

My intention for this book was for it to be a practical guide, your companion through your current and future jobs so that you can leave the legacy that you wish to.

You have worked on:

- Leaving a note for yourself when you began reading.
- Considering whether you are achievement or legacy focused.
- Discovering your rudder or your motivation to keep you going.

- Considering the organisational culture prior to making changes.
- Finding your corporate voice for all things organisational culture.
- Defining your desired culture and how to bring your people along.
- Applying the Know, Like and Trust marketing principles to embed your desired culture.
- Building a solid team.
- Leading with head, heart and backbone.
- Expanding your network to ensure you have the right people in your corner.
- Making moments that matter for your workplace.
- Defining the legacy that you wish to leave.
- Self-coaching to keep you at the top of your game when plot twists happen.
- Knowing when to quit your job and how best to pass the baton.

Think of all the positive changes you have made or are still making.

Finishing this book is just the start of you leaving a legacy.

You may well be leaving your job to go to another great opportunity, if so, use this book again.

You might have colleagues, family or friends who have seen something shift in the way you operate and the way you relate to your job. Don't keep it a secret. Gift this book to whoever needs it.

You cannot create a legacy alone. It is a collective effort, as you have now seen.

I am a firm believer in the Indian Advaita philosophy of non-duality. You are me, and I am you. Know that you will never walk alone. Leaving a legacy is typically seen as an individual pursuit. However, this book aims to shift that perspective by highlighting the collective nature of legacy-building. I'm confident it has equipped you with practical strategies to leave your mark in the workplace.

This book is going to be your guide for a few years, for many jobs to come, for the many people that you will gift this book to.

You are more than a worker – far more. Work is one piece of your life that has taken up a lot of time and I hope this book has made your work life more joyous and fulfilling.

I wrote this book for you so that you could explore your full potential at work.

By now, my voice may well be in your head. Let's go back to your voice. Return to the start of the book and read what you wrote about why you began to read this book and what your original thinking was regarding your legacy goal.

Well done on getting here!

Before we depart, have a read of this fictional case study of John who read this book and applied all of the learnings.

Fictional Case Study: John's Journey to Creating a Meaningful Legacy

John was a seasoned executive at a large not-for-profit organisation. Despite his success, he felt something was missing. This is John's journey through the twelve chapters of Making Work Meaningful: How To Create A Culture That Leaves A Legacy.

1. The Missing Piece – The Achievement and Legacy Paradox

John had climbed the corporate ladder swiftly, achieving accolades and promotions. Yet he felt unfulfilled. Recognising the achievement and legacy paradox, John realised that his accomplishments alone were not enough. He needed to focus on the legacy he wanted to leave behind.

2. Discovering Your Rudder – Your Underlying Purpose

To align his actions with his vision, John delved into discovering his rudder – his underlying purpose. He reflected on his core values, developed soft skills and learned about what truly motivated him. John realised that his passion was fostering creativity and growth in others. This purpose became the foundation of his leadership ethos.

3. Designing Your Legacy Goal

John took a step back to design his legacy goal. He asked himself what long-term impact he wanted to have on his team and the organisation. He envisioned a workplace where innovation thrived, and employees felt valued and empowered. This goal became his guiding star.

4. Defining Your Desired Culture

John understood the importance of defining a desired culture. He gathered his team to discuss the values and behaviours they wanted to see in their workplace. They collaboratively defined a culture that prioritised innovation, respect, and continuous learning.

5. Effectively Conveying Your Desired Culture

To embed this culture, John employed the Know, Like, and Trust marketing principles. He communicated the vision consistently, engaged his team through regular dialogues, and built trust by leading by example. This approach ensured that the desired culture resonated throughout the organisation.

6. Building a Solid Team

John recognised that a solid team was crucial to achieving his vision. He focused on team-building activities, addressing burnout, and fostering a collaborative environment. By delegating effectively and encouraging open communication, John built a team that was cohesive and motivated.

7. Building Alliances

Understanding the power of alliances, John actively built professional networks. He collaborated with other leaders, sought mentors, and encouraged his team to do the same. These alliances provided valuable support and resources, furthering their collective goals.

8. Leading with Head, Heart, and Backbone

John balanced logic, empathy, and courage in his leadership. He made decisions based on data (head), showed genuine concern for his team (heart), and stood firm on his principles (backbone). This balanced approach earned him respect and loyalty from his team.

9. Culture Optimisation Beyond Surveys

John went beyond traditional surveys to optimise the culture. He focused on psychological contracts – the unwritten expectations between the company and its employees. By creating moments that mattered and addressing individual needs, John nurtured a positive and resilient culture.

10. Managing Plot Twists

John's journey wasn't without challenges. When unexpected changes arose, he managed these plot twists by staying flexible and focused on his legacy goal. He viewed each challenge as an opportunity to reinforce the desired culture and support his team through transitions.

11. Knowing When to Leave and Pass the Baton

After years of dedicated leadership, John recognised when it was time to move on. He developed a comprehensive knowledge transfer plan, ensuring his successors were well-prepared to continue his work. John's departure was smooth, and his legacy was secure.

12. The Show Will Go On

Even after John left, his legacy continued to thrive. The culture he had built endured, and the team he had nurtured flourished. His commitment to making work meaningful had created a lasting impact that resonated beyond his tenure.

The Brilliant Ending

John's fictional journey is a testament to the power of intentional leadership.

By addressing each chapter of this book, he transformed not only his own experience but also the lives of those he led. His story is one of inspiration, showing that with the right focus and dedication, any leader can leave a legacy that continues to shine.

You too can make work meaningful and create a culture that leaves a lasting legacy like John did! Just follow the guide of this book.

The steps you take today will shape the legacy you leave tomorrow. Make each action count, stay true to your vision, and create a culture that resonates with purpose. Share your journey with others and inspire them to create their own lasting impact.

Your legacy begins now. Let it be meaningful, let it be profound, and let it be shared with the world.

Let's make work meaningful and create cultures that leave legacies together. If John could do it, so can you.

Remember to reach out, tag me, or share your stories. I can't wait to celebrate your successes and the positive change you bring.

Activity: Reflective Questions on Ongoing Legacy

Use these questions to reflect on the ongoing impact of your legacy:

- How will my contributions continue to influence others?
- What systems and processes can I put in place to ensure my legacy endures?
- How can I support and mentor others to continue my work?
- What can I do now to ensure a lasting impact?

This book is a lifelong tool for your career. It can be applied to the future jobs that you move to. Just read this book again or do the activities for your next job. Kind of like an eat, sleep, repeat pattern with a new lens when you need it again in your next job. Using the pass-it-on mentality, if you feel anyone would benefit from reading this book, do gift it to them.

Chapter Recap

In this final chapter, we've explored the continuation of your legacy. By reflecting on your ongoing impact and putting systems in place to ensure your legacy endures, you can create a meaningful and lasting contribution to the workplace. The book started with exploring a common yet often unspoken feeling: the sense that something is missing even after achieving career success. I hope this book has enabled you to address that and more!

Your Actions:

- Reflect on the ongoing impact of your legacy.
- Implement strategies to ensure your legacy endures.
- Read all the notes you took while reading this book.
- Celebrate your journey and continue to strive for meaningful work.
- If you are working on your progress, continue on with the work. Don't stop until you are done.
- Contact Prina to let her know how this book has served you. Prina's details are on the last page.

Notes:

Acknowledgements

Writing a book has been one of the hardest things I have done. I could not have done it without the support of many people. There are some people who I want to say a particular thank you to for being there for me.

Lindsay – thank you for loving, feeding and watering me. I did it!

Mum – thank you for peeling and deseeding millions of pomegranates for me and for everything.

Polly - thank you for holding the UK fort whenever I am in need, sister.

Jitesh – Kuthri, I told you I would do it.

Manisha – you are always on my mind and I can't wait to meet Aman.

My friends – I love you long time. Thanks for being there from the beginning.

My blood and chosen family - I am a very lucky person to have you in my life!

My book buddies and fellow entrepreneurs who you must look up: Leanne Hughes, Mel Loy, Chris Fenning, Dave Pullan, Robbie Samuels and Chloe Temple - my book inspiration buddies and 'friendtors'. What a ride. Jade Miller a HUGE thanks to you for enabling me to get it all together.

My Early Readers - I appreciate all your feedback on this book. Alyce Persich, Genein, Sophie Of The Sophie Co Group, Priya Shah, Jill Dixon, Chris Gollow (the Robin to my Batman), Bethan Winn,

Bec Chamberlain, Jas Shergill, Liz Spina (and Hilly), Deanne, Garry Fisher, Suzzi Nizich, Kristel Clark, Nicola Veal, Natalie Hope, Elena Lennox, James Coomber, Stephen Giles, Vanessa Broughton, Anselmo Martinez, Kirsty Officer, Freya Barr, Natalie Fletcher, Fiona Norling, Kaila Carmichael, Mel Loy, Ryan Hall, Kieran Johnson, Leanne Hughes, Kate Thomson, Jesvin Karimi, Lisa Williams, Rebecca Elder, Rachel Okazaki, Nita Jane, Kiru Thangadurai, Aleisha Santoriello, Samta Thakrar, Chloe Temple and Susan Paczkowski.

Dave Foxall my editor – I appreciate the feedback, humour and I will come visit you in Barcelona sometime!

Kelly Irving and the Expert Author Community – thank you for the support and showing me the way.

Rob Fitzpatrick and his Write Useful Books Community – I reckon this is a useful book thanks to all I learned from you.

My clients – thank you for trusting in me to test out all of what is covered in this book on you. I am deeply grateful.

Anyone who met with me to "nut out" my thoughts.

And, to YOU, the reader - I did it for you.

Ways to Work with Prina

My Approach:

If we work together we are guaranteed to learn a lot, find ways to change your workplace for the better, and we will also have a few laughs along the way.

I work with clients in a partnership manner. I prefer to work with you long term as change takes time.

If I am working with you as a one off, I am sure to leave you with plenty of material to focus on after our time together – I don't want to be a one-hit wonder.

Workshops:

I love facilitating topical sessions and developing your workforce. Whether it be working with your executives, leaders, teams or people. I am seasoned at handling the most difficult subjects with respect and care. I have worked on executive group coaching, leadership and people development projects, you name it.

Consulting:

I can consult on most things linked to the stages of the employee life cycle. I enjoy taking on projects that will enable decent ways to change the workplace.

Speaking and MCing at Your Event:

I have a lot to say. You may have already tuned in to my Ways to Change the Workplace Podcast. If not, do subscribe! Speaking is something I love to do as it enables aha moments for your people. I often weave in sociology and social psychology concepts to my speeches and will leave you with plenty of food for thought.

Connect with me:

Email: prina@prinashah.com to tell me how you went with this book

Sign up to my newsletter to gain practical insights and tools for how to make work more meaningful: https://www.prinashah.com/signup

Visit for more resources from the book: https://www.makeworkmeaningful.shop/

I am on LinkedIn which is more my office: www.linkedin.com/in/prinashah/

Find me on Instagram – which is more my playground and I use it as a bit of a visual diary of my business escapades: www.instagram.com/prina.shah/

Subscribe to The Ways to Change the Workplace Podcast: Learn how to make effective change in the areas that you need to address at work. https://www.waystochangetheworkplace.com/

Join My Ways to Change the Workplace private Facebook group with hundreds of others: https://www.facebook.com/groups/waystochangetheworkplace

Extra Notes:

www.ingramcontent.com/pod-product-compliance
Lightning Source LLC
Chambersburg PA
CBHW072156070526
44585CB00015B/1169